SAIL & STEAM

SAIL & STEAM
A Century of Maritime Enterprise: 1840-1935
Photographs from The National Maritime Museum, Greenwich

John Falconer

·DRG·

David R. Godine
Publisher
BOSTON

First published in the United States by
DAVID R. GODINE, PUBLISHER, INC.
Horticultural Hall
300 Massachusetts Avenue
Boston, Massachusetts 02115

ISBN 0-87923-995-6
LC 93-78972

First edition
Printed in Italy

Frontispiece:
The barque *Penang* in the Britannia Dry Dock, Millwall, 1932
Photograph by Russell Westwood
Looming over the back gardens of West Ferry Road from her berth in
the Britannia Dry Dock, this view of the *Penang* vividly illustrates the
former pervasive influence of the sea in British life: today the dock itself
has long since been filled in and London's river traffic is no more than a
pale shadow of pre-war days. Built as the *Albert Rickmers* in 1905, the
Penang was one of the last of the big sailing ships: she survived up until
the Second World War, but in December 1940 she was torpedoed in the
North Atlantic by a German U-boat and lost with all hands.

CONTENTS

. . . England, where men and sea interpenetrate, so to speak – the sea entering into the life of most men, and the men knowing something or everything about the sea, in the way of amusement, of travel, or of breadwinning.

Joseph Conrad, *Youth: A Narrative* (1898)

There dwells a wife by the Northern Gate
And a wealthy wife is she;
She breeds a breed of roving men
And casts them over sea.

And some are drowned in deep water,
And some in sight o'shore,
And word goes back to the weary wife
And ever she sends more.

Rudyard Kipling, *The Sea-Wife* (1893)

INTRODUCTION

Addressing a meeting of the British Association in April 1891, the veteran traveller and photographer John Thomson gave a ringing declaration of faith in the importance of photography as a recorder of history's onward march. Looking back on the great figures of history, he bemoaned the lack of accurate images of their features and the world in which they lived. But at last technology had caught up with the great feats of the human spirit, and at the high noon of Victorian endeavour photography was on hand to bear witness to the inexorable surge of achievement: 'We are now making history, and the sun picture supplies a means of passing down a record of what we are, and what we have achieved in this nineteenth century of our progress.' The art and science of photography was half a century old when Thomson made these remarks and the industrial nations of the world were climbing towards a peak of maritime and economic expansion. In the minds of men like Thomson, the camera's impartial eye, guided and controlled by the skill and discrimination of the photographer, would serve to document this growth, the industries and triumphs, the men of mark and a civilizing mission to the world at large.

The invention of photography in 1839, within a few years of the inception of the Victorian era, coincided with (and was itself a product of) the birth of an age of optimism and growth: imperial expansion and industrial development were but two aspects of a vigorous society that demanded a witness to its onward march, and the camera was a tool ideally suited to supply the age with an image of itself. The literal accuracy of the camera (leaving aside the interpretative function of the operator) was tailor-made to reflect the accomplishments of these busy and materialistic decades. And nowhere is this more vividly illustrated than in the photographer's documentation of maritime themes, from the most elevated and formal to the most intimate and domestic. Maritime traditions and heritage were a source of continual pride during the nineteenth century: the sea carried trade, was a bountiful larder and, not least, provided a protective bulwark against national enemies. And the surviving photographic record is perhaps the most potent legacy of just how deeply the sea has permeated every aspect of national life, from the grand spectacle of fleet reviews to the humble pleasures of holidays by the sea.

Photography was also on hand to supply visual testimony to the march of history and material progress, particularly in its documentation of the immense technical advances in the fields of industry and engineering which so characterized the nineteenth century. In 1854 Joseph Cundall was approached by the shipbuilder John Scott Russell to take two views each month recording the progress of the construction of Brunel's *Great Eastern* at Millwall. To modern eyes these precisely composed views seem to emphasize the heroic quality of the undertaking, but it is worth noting the more prosaic impetus behind the record, which was to satisfy Brunel as to progress in the building of the great ship. In addition, the very constraints of the medium offer a telling metaphor of industrial endeavour. While the early technology of large-format photography – conducted with complicated chemistry, bulky equipment and requiring long exposures – was such that poses were stiff and formal, these very limitations direct our attention to the massive structures of iron and steel rising from the stocks: blurred and insubstantial figures, dwarfed by the structures beside which they stand, serve to emphasize the immense solidity of the material advances of the Victorian age.

The photography of maritime subjects in dockyards and harbours fitted neatly into the mainstream of the expanding field of commercial photography, and such documentation continued unabated throughout the nineteenth century. Such firms as the architectural photographers Bedford Lemère undertook numerous commissions to record the building of great luxury liners such as the *Aquitania*, and these meticulous large-format studies powerfully evoke the elegance of a vanished age of travel. Photography too supplies perhaps the most graphic images of the might of the great battleships that secured and maintained naval hegemony over large parts of the globe, particularly evident in the extensive series of views showing the construction of the revolutionary HMS *Dreadnought* from the laying of the keel to her launch in 1906. Further afield, photographers more used to tourists as customers were also quick to capitalize on the photographic potential of great marine engineering projects, whether for their compositional qualities or as sources of patriotic pride. Thus the Port Said based business of Arnoux Frères produced in the early 1870s an extensive series of views of the recently completed Suez Canal, while in Australia the Sydney photographer Charles Percy Pickering produced some fine studies of Circular Quay in 1870 as part of his work as official photographer to the Metropolitan Intercolonial Exhibition. And in Ceylon the firm of Skeen & Co. proudly recorded the building of the massive breakwater which upon completion in 1885 greatly increased the commercial capacity of Colombo harbour.

But even before these early industrial applications, some photographers had from the earliest days been attracted to the medium as a means of artistic expression, seeing the photographic print as a worthy successor to the painted image, uniting creative vision with the camera's fidelity in recording the objective world. And one man in particular sought to extend photography's artistic borders to include maritime themes. A talented watercolour artist specializing in maritime subjects, the Reverend Richard Calvert Jones was a friend of the father of English photography, William Henry Fox Talbot, and in the early 1840s he abandoned painting for the camera, taking some of the earliest maritime photographs. While his work supplies the historian with a wealth of technical information about mid nineteenth-century shipping, his primary purpose was artistic, a fact amply demonstrated in his close-up studies of rigging, compositions which are purely graphic in conception and execution.

But Jones is perhaps one of those exceptional figures to whom the description 'marine photographer' can reasonably be applied. By and large the term is difficult to justify as a description of a distinct group of photographers defined by their use of the sea as a subject, or by any particular sensitivity to maritime subjects. Jones had come to photography after many years as a talented marine watercolourist and he transferred many of his artistic preoccupations to his photographic work. But for the majority of commercial photographers maritime themes were of no greater or lesser significance than work they might be called upon to produce in other fields. That such a photographic tradition, sharing the concerns of contemporary marine painters, could not have been expected to develop is no doubt due in part to the technical limitations of early photography. Those very aspects of the marine environment which have so attracted painters over the centuries – the grandeur of a ship under full sail, the excitement of naval actions, the romantic power and destructive violence of the sea – were not available to photography, which for the first fifty years of its existence at least was essentially a recorder of static scenes, carefully composed views selected for those moments when movement of wind or tide would not destroy that clarity and precision which was at the heart of photography's magic. And while the bulk of the output of a number of photographers consisted of broadly maritime subjects, this was as often as not no more than a response to their location in a busy port. The work of such photographers is often of a high standard and forms a valuable historical record of ship types, construction methods and harbour life, but it is not necessarily informed by any specific sensitivity to the sea. The work of many photographers based in the great ports of the world falls into this category: West and Company of Portsmouth, Richard Ellis of Malta, Stretton of Calcutta (even though he specifically advertised himself as a 'marine photographer'), all form part of that honourable band of commercial operators who produced documentary records of considerable importance and merit, but whose talents could be – and often were – directed with equal facility to other subjects and themes.

Only a very few photographers have created a body of work based on maritime themes that transcends pure documentation and, through a particular sensitivity to the subject and an individual point of view, evokes a deep and personal sense of man's relationship with the sea. Lesser photographers occasionally achieve such results by skill and good fortune, and there are many such happy instances in the following pages, but only the most skilled and sensitive can consistently evoke a sense of time and place. Here the sense of a personal viewpoint is critical. Frank Meadow Sutcliffe's documentation of the life of the port of Whitby in the last quarter of the nineteenth century is one example: picturesque urchins and gnarled fishermen, the harbour at dusk, all these elements of real life are used in the photographs to call up a vision of Whitby which, while retaining its photographic accuracy, creates an intensely personal interpretation of the port and its daily life.

A harsher but equally individual vision of man's relationship with the sea can be seen in the work of the Gibson family, whose members have for more than a century recorded life along the always dangerous and often treacherous coasts of the extreme south-western tip of England. John Gibson, the founder of the firm, had started his life at sea, but became interested in photography in the early 1860s and by 1866 had set himself up as a professional photographer. From that time until the present day succeeding generations have been based either on the Scilly Islands or on the mainland at Penzance, photographing all aspects of life but becoming particularly celebrated for their pictures of the shipwrecks that are such a common feature of these coasts. Few major disasters in the area have escaped their cameras in the past century, most of them views taken in the days following a wrecking, often with spectators gathered on surrounding clifftops. These pictures, both individually and as a group, achieve a melancholy beauty in their illustration of human endeavour brought low by the raw power and violence of the sea. Other, more subversive, comments also have their place in these images: the carefully arranged group of sightseers aiming their telescopes at the wreck in the bay forms not only a nicely calculated compositional balance, but illustrates the unfailing human appetite for disaster (and also perhaps offers an incidental and ironic commentary on the ambivalent role played by the photographer as chronicler and observer of life's dramas and tragedies).

Other nineteenth- and early twentieth-century photographers were equally skilled technicians, but in most cases the demands of straight documentation, rather than personal expression, were uppermost. The work of Francis Frith and Company, while never falling below the highest professional standards, enters into this category. The views by Frith that are included in this book were taken around the turn of the century, when the company was engaged in producing a comprehensive series of views of the landscape and topography of all the major cities and towns of Great Britain. There is little doubt that the resulting photographs, while all issued under the name of the founder of the firm, were taken by various anonymous employees, and while an overall compositional style is discernible, there is no great feeling of the individual behind the camera. The images remain, however, invaluable records of people, places and events for ever gone. The work of Frederick S. Gould of Gravesend falls into a similar category. In the last quarter of the nineteenth century and into the present century, this firm produced thousands of pictures of sailing ships and steamers moored at Gravesend preparatory to setting sail. Taken as a whole, this body of work forms a rich archive of material for the maritime historian, supplying minutely detailed portraits of hundreds of vessels covering the most prosperous years of the shipping history. A more informal and human side of the firm's work is seen in the documentation of events in and around Gravesend at the turn of the century.

Amateur photographers too have made their own equally valuable contribution to the historical record, often documenting the more informal and intimate details of life passed over by their professional colleagues. Many of the most fascinating glimpses of the way of life of fishing villages, or of off-duty sailors relaxing on a ship of the Royal Navy, are the work of anonymous photographers. Oliver Hill, for instance, in the course of a long life devoted himself to photographing and researching the local craft of the British Isles, leaving a unique collection of negatives of a way of life gone for ever. The Australian Alan Villiers, meanwhile, used the camera as an adjunct to the pen, illustrating his many books on the last days of the big sailing ships with a series of evocative views of working life on board the great square-riggers.

Recognition of photography's importance as an artistic and historical resource is nowadays commonplace, but this appreciation is a relatively modern phenomenon and up until a few decades ago many institutions and libraries treated photograph collections as inconvenient white elephants, difficult to classify and of little value. The National Maritime Museum can reasonably claim to have early recognized the importance of photographs as a source of historical information, having actively collected in this field from shortly after the Second World War. All the photographs used in the present book come from the Museum's Historic Photographs Section, which now contains well in excess of half a million images in either print or negative form. In this collection will be found the work of the early masters of photography such as William Henry Fox Talbot and the Reverend Richard Calvert Jones, the photographic archives of famous shipbuilding firms such as William Denny of Dumbarton, the personal albums of naval families, topographical views of seaports around the world, and an unrivalled collection of ship portraits from the mid nineteenth century up to the present day.

This selection of images does no more than scratch the surface of such a rich resource, and makes no claim to supplying a comprehensive account of its contents: the choice of pictures has inevitably resulted in the ruthless discarding of a number of beautiful and evocative photographs. It should, however, give the reader some indication of the range and quality of material available for the documentation of our maritime past. And while no attempt has been made to present a comprehensive maritime history in photographs, the structure of the book has been organized to illustrate some of the prominent themes in our relationship with the sea, and even if a number of subjects have necessarily been omitted it is hoped that this approach will offer a certain narrative coherence without doing irreparable damage to historical balance. Any other person compiling such a book would no doubt make an entirely different selection from the wide choice available, reflecting personal interests and preferences (and no doubt prejudices), and the Museum's collections certainly contain material for further volumes. This is as it should be, for a book such as this is ultimately a witness to the skill and dedication of scores of photographers who have helped to shape our perception and bring to life our past.

GREAT DAYS OF SAIL

Changing sails on the four-masted barque *Port Jackson*, 1913
Photographer unknown

An appropriate introduction to the sailing ship age as it coincided with the early history of photography is supplied in the work of the Reverend Richard Calvert Jones, who made some of the earliest photographs of British shipping. Jones was excited by the precision of the photographic image and quickly abandoned watercolour painting in favour of the new medium. As in his paintings, he was most strongly attracted to maritime themes and in the mid 1840s produced a series of studies of shipping at Swansea. These beautifully toned images, printed from paper negatives which result in a grainy image not unlike an etching, preserved the painterly qualities of the artist's earlier work, while still taking advantage of the documentary realism of the photograph.

Long exposures required stationary subjects, and hence most of his compositions were made at low tide with the vessels grounded on the mud of the harbour floor and not

Opposite: The wreck of the *Gunvor*, 6 April 1912
Photograph by Gibson of Penzance
This three-masted steel barque was the largest ship lost to the rocks of Black Head, north-east of Mevagissey, which she struck in heavy fog with a cargo of nitrates from South America. Her loss was costly in financial rather than human terms: she was wrecked so close inshore that her crew were all able to escape by the rope ladder that can still just be seen hanging from her bowsprit.

shifting at their moorings: for the maritime historian this is an additional bonus, since it provides an unimpeded view of the form of these stout little barques and brigs before the major technological and design developments of the second half of the nineteenth century, which over the succeeding fifty years were to alter so radically the appearance of the merchant sailing ship. And it was in vessels such as these that an overwhelming proportion of the nation's seaborne trade was carried up to the middle years of the nineteenth century. We may look at these ships today through the eyes of romance and nostalgia, but these were vessels built for the most down-to-earth reason of all – to make a profit – and all their physical characteristics were the result of severely practical factors, determined by available technology, legislative constraints and the economics of cargo transport.

Most immediately apparent is their boxy shape, flat bottom and great depth in relation to their length. Many British harbours at this time possessed only rudimentary docking facilities, so ships had to be able to rest on the ground in ports that dried out at low tide, and hence a flat floor was a necessity. A second major consideration was the 1773 tonnage rules under which these ships were built. These regulations provided an arcane formula for calculating the tonnage of a ship based on her length and breadth, but they did not take into account her depth except as a nominal value. Since port dues, pilotage charges and other expenses were based on tonnage, it made evident commercial sense to build ships to the greatest possible depth, thus increasing cargo capacity while registering the lowest possible tonnage. While this might have implications for her sailing qualities – such vessels were generally cumbersome and unresponsive – the drawbacks were offset by gain in cargo capacity. Such ships were labour-intensive both to build and to maintain, and represented a constant fight against decay, stress and general wear. But until the economic situation demanded it, and technological improvements were able to meet such requirements in the form of new materials and building techniques, the impetus for change was small. Indeed, although the old tonnage measurement rules were changed in 1836, and again in 1854, many builders continued to construct their ships to the old patterns for years afterwards. In fact, the massive growth in shipping tonnage which characterized the second half of the century was slow in starting. The end of the Napoleonic Wars heralded a slump in maritime trade and between 1815 and the accession of Queen Victoria in 1837, total English shipping tonnage was nearly static at a little under 3 million tons. By 1851, however, this figure had risen to 4.3 million tons.

While the second half of the nineteenth century saw the great leap forward in both demand and technology which developed the merchant sailing ship to its highest form, the same period also witnessed the parallel development of the steamship, which by the end of the century had all but superseded it. The speed of this transformation is perhaps most clearly seen if we consider that a mere two decades separate the ships in Calvert Jones's views of Swansea from the sleek and elegant clippers of the China and Australia trades, and that a further twenty years were to see the sailing ship in swift and irreversible decline in the face of the steamship. But sail fought its corner well, and as the threat of the steamship increased, so the sailing ship sought out specialized routes and cargoes where it could operate in viable economic competition with the steamer.

The middle years of the century saw a number of improvements, both legislative and technical, which set the scene for this transformation of merchant shipping. Increasing government activity in maritime legislation was in itself a sign of the pace of change and the expansion of the industry. In 1850 an act was passed 'for improving the conditions of Masters, Mates and Seamen and maintaining discipline in the Merchant Service', creating the Marine Department of the Board of Trade, which was given the responsibility for ensuring the competence of masters. The Steam Navigation Act of the

following year made further provision for the safety of sea travel, and in 1854 the Merchant Shipping Act laid out 548 clauses relating to the merchant service. In the following decade further improvements relating to training, signalling, navigation and general safety built on these foundations. Such acts were in themselves an indication of the increasing volume of both trade and passenger traffic from this time on, as colonial expansion, the discovery of gold in Australia and America, and the creation of new markets all contributed to the movement of people and goods, while the major conflicts of the Crimean War and the American Civil War fed further shipping booms in the 1850s and 1860s.

Although steam had started to play a significant role in industrial production from the late eighteenth century, particularly in the mining and textile industries, harnessing its power to drive ships efficiently required the solving of many technical and economic problems. The first practical steamship, the *Charlotte Dundas*, travelled nineteen miles along the Forth–Clyde Canal in 1803 at an average speed of six miles an hour, and in succeeding decades steam-driven paddle steamers became a common enough sight on the coastal passenger services. It was not until the latter half of the century, however, that the steamship was able to make a final and successful challenge to the sailing ship on the longer trade routes. The major reasons for this relate to technical developments, and little progress was made until a more efficient alternative was found to the paddle as a means of propulsion. The development of screw propulsion from the late 1830s partially solved this problem, but introduced some of its own. The stresses imposed on a wooden hull by the vibration of the engine and the torque of the shaft hindered the development of the steam cargo vessel until the building of ships in iron became feasible on a large scale. By the 1850s, however, several yards were building ships in both iron and wood, and by 1880 in Britain only the smaller sailing ships, those under about 500 tons, were still being built of wood.

The last major factor lay in the uneconomic nature of the steam engine in its early days of shipboard use. So inefficient were these engines that the coal needed to fire the boilers left insufficient space to ship a profitable cargo. And even when steam was well established on long-distance routes, lines such as P&O relied on a large fleet of sailing vessels to carry coal to bunker stations in the Mediterranean, the Red Sea, India and the Far East. These technical issues gave the sailing ship in 'high-value' trades a breathing space that allowed for design improvements when she could have been expected to become rapidly obsolete. Only when industry became able to manufacture boilers of sufficient size and strength to deliver economical steam pressure, and engines could exploit this more efficiently, and when iron and steel could be obtained in sufficient quantity and low price to build large ships, was the steamer in a position to oust the sailing ship from the sealanes of the world. But by the 1870s the balance between wooden and iron shipping was starting to be reversed in favour of the latter, and by the 1880s this decline was irreversible. The final nail in the coffin of the sailing ship was the introduction of Siemen's steel, which made it possible after about 1878 to construct boilers that could operate at high pressures and thus with greater efficiency and lower fuel consumption. In 1881 the *Aberdeen* was built for the Australian emigrant trade. Her triple expansion engine, fed by steam generated in a Siemen's steel boiler at a hitherto unattainable pressure of 125 pounds per square inch, lowered coal consumption and was one of the factors that permitted the building of ships of 15,000 tons and more. On her maiden voyage she sailed from Plymouth to Melbourne in forty-two days, with only one coaling stop. The launching of the *Aberdeen* not only signalled the end for the large sailing ship, it additionally coincided with the end of major merchant shipbuilding on the Thames.

But there was a transitional period, in which the sailing ship was to reach its peak as a form of efficient transport, evident both in the form and the look of the merchant ship. From the middle of the century more manageable double topsails began to replace the large single sails that had previously been the norm, while the sail canvas itself and the rigging became both lighter and stronger. The later development of steel masts and rigging, coupled with economic pressures, made for smaller and more economic crews and called for different skills from mariners. Before these developments the wooden ship formed a little world of its own and in an emergency even major repairs to masts and hull would be carried out by the ship's crew with the resources available. While hands such as the sailmaker and the carpenter had their own specialized crafts, every sailor also had to be master of many skills, from steering the vessel to maintaining rigging and working aloft in conditions often both exhausting and dangerous. And on a sailing ship work was one thing of which there was never any shortage. A myriad other chores had to be completed to ensure smooth and efficient running, and the seaman's life throughout the nineteenth century was hard, dangerous and insecure. It is not surprising, therefore, that as steam came into the ascendant in the later years of the century, many sailors abandoned the

rigours of sailing ship life for the better pay, shorter voyages and less demanding duties on steamships, so that by the early years of the twentieth century, the average age of seamen on sailing ships had risen considerably as new blood became harder to attract. By the end of the century also, conditions at sea lagged behind those enjoyed by the industrial worker, both in terms of pay and conditions, although the situation slowly improved as a result of the various merchant shipping acts that came into force. Minimum requirements for such matters as diet were established, but in the end the sea will always be a harsh and dangerous world. Some statistics from the period make this graphically clear: between 1872 and 1884, for instance, an average of 3,000 seamen a year lost their lives through drowning and accidents, while in 1865 alone 2,259 seamen also died from diseases such as cholera and dysentery.

That most romantic of all sailing ship images, that of the sleek clipper racing from China to London with the new season's crop of tea, marks the apogee of fast sailing ship design in the popular imagination. Sacrificing cargo capacity for speed, these graceful ships with their sharply raked bows and lean, fine-lined hulls, driven along with a massive spread of canvas, seem to epitomize the high noon of the sailing ship in both beauty and performance. In England the clipper reached its fullest form in the 1860s, and the fine lines of these ships can be seen in the *Cutty Sark*, now preserved in dry dock at Greenwich.

But for all their beauty, grace and speed, the economic importance of this relatively short-lived phenomenon has been greatly exaggerated. It was only in the transport of certain specialized high-value commodities such as tea that speed was crucial to the extent of making it a major design factor. The clippers only ever accounted for a minute proportion of the world's sailing ship fleets, but more importantly, they were effectively obsolete even as they were being built. Steamers could make the China run more quickly than the *Cutty Sark* was ever able to do and, in addition, could bring back far larger cargoes. And only a few days before the *Cutty Sark* was launched in 1869 the Suez Canal was opened, cutting the passage to the east by some 3,000 miles and conferring yet another advantage on the steamship, since sailing vessels could not use the canal. But unlike premium cargoes such as tea, bulk goods like rice and jute could not afford the steamer freight rates (with dues in addition for using the Suez Canal), and in these trades the sailing ship still had a role to play. Like a number of other clippers, the *Cutty Sark* was transferred to the more mundane Australian wool trade in the late 1870s, in which for many years she continued to operate profitably.

But although the demise of the sailing vessel was assured by the end of the nineteenth century, the process was prolonged by several remarkable comebacks. In the mid 1880s the introduction of cheap, high-quality steel led to the building of hundreds of the big four-masted barques which were able to compete profitably with steamships until well into the 1890s. Many were over 300 feet long and could carry over 5,000 tons of cargo, and a drop of freight rates by 40 per cent between 1889 and 1895 further increased their economic viability. While the steel construction of these ships – including the masts and rigging – required the facilities of a shipyard for major repairs, they were able to rely on their strength of build in a way that the wooden ships could not. By the turn of the century this construction had largely dried up, although some of the vessels continued to sail up to the First World War and beyond. And it was the First World War that gave the merchant sailing ship another short lease of life, particularly in Canada and the United States. Freight rates rose dramatically during the conflict and old ships were refitted and pressed back into profitable service. A new building programme on both sides of the Atlantic constructed hundreds of wooden schooners to meet the new demand. But by the early 1920s the boom subsided with the drop in freight rates, and with two significant exceptions, one in Finland, the other in Germany, the era of the merchant sailing ship in Europe and America drew to a close.

Of these, the most remarkable final flowering of the sailing ship was the fleet of ships owned by Captain Gustaf Erikson and based on the Baltic port of Mariehamn in the Åland Islands. In the inter-war years, when the last of the ageing square-riggers were being slowly eased out of operation by lack of freights, rising maintenance costs, the world recession and the cargo steamer, Erikson managed to operate a profitable fleet of sailing ships, mainly in the transport of high-bulk, low-value cargoes such as timber and wheat. In the mid 1930s he owned more than twenty sailing vessels of various types, and by concentrating on those commodities where speed of delivery was not vital managed to create a financially successful enterprise which continues – in the form of motorships – to this day. The secret of Erikson's success lay partly in operating on very tight margins and partly in taking full advantage of the economic situation of the 1920s and 30s. Arguing that the majority of European and American seamen had priced themselves out of the market, he recruited his crews initially from young Åland Islanders, many of them only fifteen or sixteen years old, and kept their numbers and wages to the bare minimum. To compensate for reduced crew numbers Erikson took advantage of many labour-saving devices such as winches, and if pay was low, food was always plentiful and good. The officers were of high calibre and the Åland Islanders were natural sailors. All this made for a happy ship, and while such a small and young crew meant hard work for all, morale was good.

Erikson himself had spent all his life on sailing ships and was, in Alan Villiers's words, 'a small man with a limp and a somewhat aggressive way of speaking . . . [who] had two great and opposing ambitions – one that his ships should be kept up magnificently, and the other, that no money should be spent on them'. A small additional income was also earned by taking on a few hands, usually Europeans or Americans, who paid for the privilege of working their passage; for in a final irony, as sail died away its romance and attraction became more potent to a young generation. But even this could not long delay the inevitable and by the late 1940s, when the final sailing voyages were made by Erikson ships, even they could not be run profitably. The days of the big sailing traders were finally over, and while the march of progress brings its own rewards, it is difficult not to echo the sense of loss at their demise expressed in John Masefield's couplet:

> They mark our passage as a race of men,
> Earth will not see such ships as those agen.

***Opposite above:* Ships taking the ground at Swansea, 1840s**
Photograph by the Reverend Richard Calvert Jones
This very early maritime image, taken on a paper negative in the mid 1840s, shows two typical merchant sailing ships grounded on the mud of the River Tawe. The ship on the left is the *Mary Dugdale*, built at Kingston-upon-Hull in 1835; she was probably one of the Swansea copper fleet that brought the ore across the Atlantic from Cuba and South America.

***Opposite below:* Brig at Swansea, 1840s**
Photograph by the Reverend Richard Calvert Jones
The brig lying with a topsail schooner alongside in the shingle at Swansea has not been identified, but this photograph offers one of the earliest and clearest views of a merchant ship of the period, showing her deck fittings and rigging in sharpest detail. Like many merchant ships at that time, the vessels in both these photographs have painted ports along their hulls in imitation of warships.

Below: **Harvey's Shipyard, Littlehampton, *c*. 1900**
Photographer unknown
Posed in front of a vessel under construction, John Harvey, the yard's owner, stands with his workforce of shipwrights and labourers; the younger figures in the front row are apprentices ser-ving their seven-year term. Many such small shipyards, generally family concerns, survived well into the present century. Their technological requirements were relatively modest and would have encompassed a sawpit, mould loft, blacksmith's shop and steambox for shaping hull planking.

Opposite above: **The *Parramatta* on the stocks,
Sunderland, May 1866**
Photograph by Paul Stabler
The *Parramatta* is seen in Sir James Laing's shipyard shortly before her launch. Laing was a pioneer of iron shipbuilding on the River Wear, and built his first iron vessel there in 1853. It is indicative of the uneven transition from wood to iron and steel, however, that the *Parramatta*, the last wooden ship to be built in Laing's yard, was not launched until 1866, more than twenty years after the construc-tion of the iron-hulled *Great Britain* in 1843.

Opposite below: **The iron ship *Ranee* under repair, 1870s**
Photographer unknown
Built in 1864 as the *Cowasjee Jehangeer*, the *Ranee* is seen here having some of the iron plates of her hull replaced after a collision. Despite its heavier weight by volume than wood, the greater strength of iron allowed lighter and bigger ships with increased cargo capacity to be built.

Opposite above: **The crew of the *Wild Deer*, c. 1880**
Photographer unknown
This group portrait of the crew of the *Wild Deer* illustrates well the ornate carved work and figurehead with which the bows of many merchant ships were embellished. The *Wild Deer*, a three-masted ship of wood on an iron frame, was built at Glasgow in 1863. She was one of the earliest ships to be fitted with double topsails in place of the large and cumbersome single topsails and she survived until 1883, when she was driven ashore on North Rock, County Down, and became a total loss.

Opposite below: **Captain William Cassady, master of the *Greta*, with family and crew, Port Pirie, Australia, c. 1885**
Photographer unknown
The group posed in this domestic scene on the poop of the *Greta* includes Cassady's wife Margaret, seated with their daughter Janet, other crew members and visitors from ashore. Margaret Cassady was pregnant when this photograph was taken, but died on the voyage home shortly after giving birth to a second daughter.

Above: **A. G. Traill, ship's carpenter, 1900s**
Photographer unknown
An impressive representative of that last generation of seamen whose whole working lives were spent in sailing ships, Traill was born in the early 1840s and was still actively employed as a ship's carpenter on board the *Port Jackson* in 1913.

Opposite: **The four-masted barque *Hougomont* c. 1920**
Photographer unknown
The *Hougomont* was one of the big steel sailing ships which in the 1890s made a last challenge to the growing supremacy of steam. Built at Greenock in 1897, she became part of Gustaf Erikson's fleet after the First World War and worked the Australia run until 1933.

Right: **Helmsman of the *Illawarra*, 1890s**
Photographer unknown
A required skill of every seaman was proficiency at steering the ship in all conditions. The two-hour stretch which comprised each turn at the wheel called for both skill and physical stamina, since to drift off course in a sailing ship could result in serious damage aloft and danger below.

Below: **Cadets taking sextant readings on board the four-masted barque *Port Jackson*, 1913**
Photographer unknown
By the early 1900s opportunities for training on sailing ships were becoming increasingly scarce. The firm of Devitt and Moore therefore purchased several sailing vessels specifically to train cadets in seamanship. The *Port Jackson* was taken over for this purpose in 1906 and carried up to 100 cadets, as well as her cargo.

The four-masted barque *Medway* under sail, 1912
Photographer unknown
The *Medway*, built in 1902, was another vessel used by Devitt and Moore as a sail training ship for cadets. This view, taken during a passage from New York to Adelaide, shows the crew working on the deck in rough weather. This tiring and dangerous labour in heavy seas was made more perilous by the volume of dead water running across the deck as the ship rolled.

Crew members of the barque *Fahrwohl*, c. 1910

Photograph probably by James Randall

Crew members pose nonchalantly high above the deck on the main-mast of the Finnish barque *Fahrwohl*. Built on the Clyde in 1892, the *Fahrwohl* had a productive career carrying cargoes of timber, grain and nitrates to Europe from the ports of North and South America. Her working life spanned more than three decades and she was finally broken up at Wilhelmshaven in 1924.

Opposite above: **Changing sails on the *Parma*, 1932–3**

Photograph by Alan Villiers

This photograph, taken from the foretop of the four-masted barque *Parma*, shows crew members engaged in the arduous task of changing the mainsail during the voyage between Port Victoria and Falmouth with a cargo of grain.

Opposite below: **The three-masted ship *Af Chapman* leaving Plymouth, 1929**

Photographer unknown

Built at Whitehaven as the *Dunboyne* and launched in 1888, this ship sailed on the Australian run for many years. In 1923 she was bought by the Swedish Crown for use as a naval sail training ship and was re-named after the celebrated eighteenth-century naval architect. Although paid off as a sail training vessel in 1937, the *Af Chapman* is still afloat as a tourist hostel in Stockholm.

The wreck of the *Hansy*, 13 November 1911

Photograph by Gibson of Penzance

The *Hansy* was sailing from Sweden to Melbourne with a cargo of pig-iron and timber when she was wrecked in Housel Bay near Lizard Point. Attempting to come about in a gale, she missed stays and was driven helplessly on to the rocks. Her loss was the culmination of a series of misfortunes that had dogged the ship since her construction in 1885. Low morale and absconding crews had been a recurring feature of her voyages, and on one occasion in 1896 she was picked up in the Bass Strait with the captain drowned and the chief officer dead by his own hand. Her end did bring some profit to the area, however, and for months afterwards there was a thriving local trade in salvaged timber.

***Opposite:* Mass burial at St Keverne of passengers from the *Mohegan*, October 1898**

Photograph by Gibson of Penzance

Gibson's compelling photograph strips away the excitement of shipwreck to expose the human tragedy. The loss of the *Mohegan* on only her second voyage remains one of the mysteries of the sea. She struck the Manacle rocks east of the Lizard promontory at full speed on 14 October 1898, just as her passengers were sitting down to dinner. In ten minutes she had disappeared with the loss of 196 lives. Navigational error may have been responsible, but all those who might have shed light on the incident died.

Opposite above: **The St Agnes lifeboat going to the assistance of the *Ardencraig*, 8 January 1911**
Photograph by Francis Mortimer
This rare photograph of a lifeboat in action shows the *Charles Deere James* pulling towards the *Ardencraig* off the Isles of Scilly. Carrying

a cargo of grain from Melbourne to Cardiff, the *Ardencraig* was 101 days out with a crew of thirty-one when a combination of fog and the northward current took her on to the Gunner rocks. The crew was rescued without loss of life, but the *Ardencraig* heeled over and sank shortly after this photograph was taken.

Opposite below: **The Dover lifeboat, *c.* 1909**
Photographer unknown
Life-saving societies started to be formed from the 1770s. These local bodies were brought under the umbrella of a single organization in 1824, and this in turn became the Royal National Lifeboat Institution in 1860. The men on parade in this boat, probably the *Mary Hamer Hoyle*, are taking part in a fund-raising collection. On some occasions during an emergency it was necessary to transport the lifeboat a considerable distance on shore, and the carriage on which this boat rests is the standard design adopted for that purpose after 1864.

Above: **Lowestoft lifeboatmen, *c.* 1900**
Photographer unknown
A Lifeboat Society had been established at Lowestoft as early as 1800. Some of the figures in this remarkable group portrait, taken inside the shed of the Lowestoft Old Company, were involved with saving life at sea for over half a century. Seen from left to right are William Hook (aged seventy-five), James Burwood (aged seventy-six), Thomas Coleman (aged eighty) and Matthew Coleman (aged eighty-one). The most famous of these, William Hook, had been a lifeboatman from the age of sixteen and had twice been awarded medals for courage by the Lifeboat Institution.

The wreck of the *Granite State*, 4 November 1895
Photograph by Gibson of Penzance
The violence and power of the sea had always been a popular artistic subject, and the photographer was able to cater for this fascination while at the same time adding a new dimension of immediacy and documentary accuracy. The *Granite State*, an American ship built in 1877, was *en route* from Falmouth to Swansea with a cargo of wheat from the River Plate when she struck on the Runnelstone, three miles south-east of Land's End. She was hauled off and towed to the shelter of Porthcurno Bay. But here she settled rapidly and when her cargo of wheat started to swell and burst her hatches, the crew took to the boats. Sightseers had only a few days to view the grounded ship, as she was soon broken up by savage winter storms.

The wooden six-masted schooner *Fort Laramie*
Photographer unknown
Constructed in 1919 by Kruse and Banks at North Bend, Oregon, the *Fort Laramie* was one of the last generation of the big American schooners, built to take advantage of the high freight rates offered during the First World War.

Opposite: **Building the *Rachel W. Stevens*, Bath, Maine, 1898**
Photographer unknown
These two photographs show the four-masted schooner under construction in the yard of the New England Company near the mouth of the Kennebec River. The expansion of the coal trade on the east coast of America in the last years of the nineteenth century led to increased demands for bigger schooners. Inadequate transport facilities, however, meant that the arrival of shipments of coal in the ports was often irregular and schooners, with their small crews and low overheads, were better able than steamships to survive a period of inactivity while waiting for a cargo. In the bottom picture the construction of the schooner's keelson, made from eight great baulks of timber, can be seen.

Circular Quay, Sydney, 1871

Photograph by Charles Pickering

Built by convict labour in the 1830s and 40s from the reclaimed Tank Stream estuary, Circular Quay was the commercial hub of the prosperous Sydney of the 1870s. With the discovery of gold in the 1850s and the subsequent rise in trade, Sydney's population increased sixfold to nearly half a million in the second half of the century. In this panoramic view, clippers are moored near the wool warehouses that lined the quay. The wool clipper in the centre of this photograph is the *Duke of Sutherland*, built in 1865; it was on this ship that the novelist Joseph Conrad served as an ordinary seaman in 1878–9.

Opposite: **Circular Quay, Sydney, *c.* 1905**

Photographer unknown

Steamers are now moored along the wharves occupied by sailing ships in the previous photograph. The quay had been rebuilt in the 1870s to cope with increased traffic and was further extended in the 1890s for passenger steamers. In the foreground are the ferry piers for cross-harbour traffic to Manly and Watson's Bay.

BRITAIN AND THE SEA

London lighterman, *c.* **1910**
Photographer unknown

No more graphic illustration of this country's intimate and formerly all-pervasive relationship with the sea could be asked than the photograph used as the frontispiece of this book. It shows the barque *Penang* berthed in the Britannia Dry Dock at Millwall in 1932, her bowsprit looming over the back yards of the houses of adjoining streets. Ignored by the residents of the street, she forms a natural element in the urban landscape of dockside London. In the sixty years since this photograph was taken a fundamental change has taken place in this relationship. Commercial waterborne traffic on the upper reaches of the Thames has all but disappeared, the greatest complex of docks in the world has been transformed into a financial extension of the City of London, and when the characteristic russet sails of one of the few surviving spritsail barges are seen, the sparkling and immaculate paintwork of her hull makes it immediately clear that she is not a working boat in the way of her ancestors. And similar transformations have taken place in the other port cities of Great Britain. Maritime trade, in those centres where it still flourishes, is concentrated in the great container ports like Felixstowe and Southampton. The economic endeavour continues, but for the majority of the population the sea has

receded from day-to-day consciousness in a way that would have been incomprehensible half a century ago.

But if the crowded harbours and rivers of Britain are now a thing of the past, it would be a mistake to assume that we are any less dependent on the sea in our daily lives. The sea remains the cheapest way by far of moving large quantities of merchandise over long distances, and an overwhelming proportion of both imports and exports travel to and from this country by sea. While the container revolution has made all this activity a good deal less conspicuous and the economics of bulk transport have led to the decay of many of the smaller ports and harbours, Britain remains indissolubly bonded to the maritime thread that runs through so much of her history and continues to inform her present.

Her borders defined by the sea, and separated by it from other countries, Britain has always seen herself as primarily a maritime nation. Even before she became a united kingdom the sea carried successive waves of traders and invaders to these shores, each of which to a greater or lesser extent has been absorbed into the fabric of the nation. After the collapse of the Roman Empire in the west and the departure of the legions from England in AD 410, the Vikings were the next major colonizing force, swooping down from the north from the late eighth century onwards to plunder Anglo-Saxon settlements. Beginning as invading pirates, they later settled in places as far apart as England, France and the

Opposite: Aquitania **on the stocks, Clydebank, April 1913**
Photograph by Bedford Lemère

Mediterranean. While their longships were technologically crude in comparison with the advanced rowing galleys of the Mediterranean, they too contributed to the development of the European sailing ship, and echoes of the form of the Viking longship were still to be seen in the local craft of the Shetland Islands up until recent years.

Although medieval trade was dominated by the great trading city states of the Mediterranean, particularly Venice, England was strategically placed to benefit from shipping passing from the Mediterranean to northern Europe and the Baltic ports. While not at this time of the same importance as Bruges, which took the cream of the north–south traffic, the foundations were being laid for London's future dominance. Maritime trade in the more northerly ports of Europe was largely controlled by the network of German cities that formed the Hanseatic League and which, at the height of its powers in the fourteenth and fifteenth centuries, stimulated and controlled seaborne commerce. The presence of merchants of the Hanseatic League in London (and to a lesser extent in other English ports) was important to English trade, since it brought in goods – furs, corn, wax, and timber – which could be traded for England's only major export, wool. But until the end of the fifteenth century England had not developed a merchant fleet of any international significance, and almost half of English exports were carried on the ships of other nations. The late fifteenth century saw a decline in the monopolistic powers of the League, and for a time English trade was largely concentrated on the London–Antwerp route.

The sixteenth century, particularly from the middle years onwards, saw a massive expansion of overseas trade as Antwerp declined in importance and this country sought new markets for the sale of English goods and new items of trade. More extensive trading links were formed with Russia and the Baltic states, and the wealth of the Caribbean was aggressively contested with Spain. By the early seventeenth century a new breed of English mariners, spurred on by reports of the vast wealth of the Indies, was sailing to capture the spice trade of the east. All these forays into the wider world were at the expense of European competitors, and this rivalry inevitably had its effect in stimulating the creation of a stronger naval force. But in the short-distance carrying trade between the ports of Europe, much of the tonnage even as late as 1600 was being carried by foreign ships, mainly Dutch. In the 1590s, for instance, seven out of eight ships carrying coal out of Newcastle were foreign, and a similar situation obtained in the movement of timber and grain. A

major turning point for the English mercantile economy came in the form of the Navigation Act of 1651, which confined trade with the English colonies to English ships, and allowed foreign ships to import only the goods of their own country into England. The act was one of the principal causes of the First Anglo-Dutch War of 1652–4, which in its turn was to England's advantage, for the end of that war saw England in possession of a huge quantity of Dutch merchant ships which could be used in the carrying trade to take advantage of the Navigation Act.

As well as being the centre of government, London was also a great shipbuilding port, constructing ships for the companies trading to the Levant, the East Indies and the Caribbean, and the seventeenth century saw a huge increase in her population and economic power. But the following century also saw the dramatic rise of the west coast ports of Bristol and Liverpool. Bristol had been a great medieval centre, but it had stagnated in later years as trade was diverted to London. With wealth accumulated from the slave trade and with the growth of colonial trade, however, Bristol prospered again and for the first half of the eighteenth century became, in Daniel Defoe's words, 'the greatest, the richest, and the best port of trade in Great Britain, London only excepted'. Particularly powerful in the codfish trade and in the import of sugar and tobacco from the West Indies, much of Bristol's wealth was a result of its independence from London, for the city authorities made sure that imports brought back to England by Bristol ships returned to Bristol. In Defoe's opinion Bristol's only disadvantages were its situation, and 'the tenacious folly of its inhabitants' in preventing any but freemen of the city from trading there. And indeed, by the 1750s Bristol was being overtaken by Liverpool, which had also profited from sugar and tobacco imports but which had come to rely mainly on the hugely profitable slave trade, which flourished until the Act of 1807 which banned the passage of slaves in British ships. These were the days of the 'triangular passage', as the slave ships sailed to the Guinea coast of West Africa to purchase slaves in exchange for cloth, firearms and other goods. The second leg took the human cargo, packed in unbelievably squalid and inhumane conditions, to the West Indies, where the slaves were sold to pay for sugar, or to Virginia, where a cargo of tobacco would be laded. Sugar and tobacco were in demand not only in England, but throughout Europe, and these commodities thus became the basis for a thriving re-export trade. In the space of little more than a century England had established herself as the greatest trading nation in Europe. Early industrialization, and ultimate victory in the long struggle with France for colonial and commercial supremacy at the end of the eighteenth century, in their turn laid the foundations of a trading supremacy that was to subsist for the whole of the nineteenth century and profoundly affected the way the English viewed themselves and the world.

This huge increase in maritime trade, particularly in the nineteenth century, has left its indelible mark on Britain's coast and river landscape. For as the maritime economy grew, it made huge demands for harbour space and docks, shipbuilding yards and cargo handling facilities. Many ports in the seventeenth and eighteenth centuries had been extended by the building of piers to enclose greater areas of water, but most of the major commercial ports were situated on rivers where this was not a practical option. Congested ports cost money both in time lost and in damage to vessels, and therefore improved dock and mooring facilities were urgently required. The first wet dock in England had been built for the fitting out of East Indiamen on the Thames at Blackwall in about 1660, and the Howland Great Wet Dock at Rotherhithe followed between 1697 and 1700. It was on the Mersey foreshore at Liverpool, however, with its expanding West Indian trade, that the first extensive series of wet docks were constructed between 1715 and the 1830s. But if London was relatively late in developing such facilities, she was finally to possess the most extensive dock system in the country. By the end of the eighteenth century, congestion in the river had reached the point where services to shipping were seriously affected. Storage for off-loaded goods was quite inadequate and merchandise was piled on the quays, sometimes for weeks, at the mercy of the weather and the remarkably expert pilferers of the Thames. The West India merchants were the first to take the situation in hand, and in 1800–1806 the West India Docks were built across the northern end of the Isle of Dogs. Between that time and the 1930s, when the London dock system reached its greatest extent, a complex network of enclosed docks, from St Katherine Dock in the west to Tilbury in the east, transformed the London river scene.

The end of the Second World War (during which the Docklands area had sustained great damage) marked a watershed in the introduction of new methods of cargo movement. Shortage of shipping space during the war had led to cargo being shipped across the Atlantic in tarred crates on the open deck, and the efficiency of this method was recalled when, around 1950, it was realized that the only way to accommodate the growing volume of world trade was to adopt some form of containerization. But it was not until 1965 that any sort of agreement on standardization was reached, and in early 1968 the first short-haul container ships to Europe started working out of Tilbury. Later the same year transatlantic trade followed, and in 1970 the first container ships began to be employed in the Australasian trade. Containerization was the major cargo-handling revolution of the century – comparable in its effects on the movement of goods to the coming of the railway – and introduced massive economies into maritime trade. Container berths could handle ten times the cargo of conventional berths with a fraction of the work-force, while turnaround was now measured in days rather than weeks. These economies of scale had their impact on the geography and viability of the older ports, since requirements of space, deepwater berths and speedy turn-around tended to make them move away from the old dock centres. Thus the trade in the old Port of London has migrated to Tilbury, Harwich and Felixstowe. As late as 1958 many of the London Docks were enjoying the busiest period of their history, but within a decade there had started the first of a series of closures and sell-offs which by the end of the 1980s left the upper reaches of the Thames almost bereft of river traffic.

In the north, major maritime centres had developed in the course of the eighteenth century. Before the Act of Union in 1702, Glasgow had little importance as a maritime centre, but with the ending of restrictions to commerce with the English colonies, a thriving trade with the eastern seaboard of America had developed by the middle years of the century. In addition to trade, the following decades saw Glasgow and the Clyde at the forefront of the new shipbuilding technology that grew out of the industrial revolution. And in this revolution the city's central role was also crucial: James Watt was mathematical instrument maker to the University in the 1760s and his construction of the first steam engine with a separate condenser, together with the area's easy access to raw materials, made the city a natural home to new scientific ideas. It was also on the Clyde that Henry Bell's first steamer *Comet* made her successful voyage in 1812, and by the end of the following year his second boat, the *Elizabeth*, was operating between Glasgow, Greenock and Helensburgh. Public response was encouraging: by 1814 nine steamers were operating on the lower Clyde and soon these sheltered waters were home to a fleet of pleasure steamers and ferries.

The growth of the Scottish shipbuilding industry and the eventual dominance of the Clyde from these small beginnings owe much to another Scottish industrial pioneer, Robert

Napier, born the son of a Dumbarton blacksmith in 1791. By the time of his death in 1876, loaded with wealth and honours, he had seen the steamship industry develop from its infancy to the building of vessels of 4,000 tons and more. His business life had started as a builder of engines for steam yachts, and as his reputation became established the East India Company commissioned him in 1836 to build the 170-foot paddle steamer *Berenice*: her sister ship, the *Atalanta*, was built and engined on the Thames. The demonstrable superiority of the Clyde-built ship over her London rival – on the first outward voyage to Bombay she was eighteen days faster than the *Atalanta* (which had to stop at Tenerife for repairs), and her engines were both more economical and functioned with much greater consistency – at a stroke established Napier as the leading shipbuilder in the country. Tenders from the Admiralty followed, and the arrival on the Clyde in 1839 of Samuel Cunard, and his subsequent association with Napier, was of great significance in the early days of Scottish shipbuilding. Cunard's idea of running a transatlantic steamship service became reality with the construction in 1840 of four Clyde-built vessels – the *Britannia*, *Acadia*, *Columbia* and *Caledonia* – all engined by Napier. The Cunard–Napier partnership is the standard case of the development of the largest scale of shipping enterprise: the simultaneous founding of a great shipping line and a great shipbuilding firm.

Nature favoured the Clyde: its great sheltered estuary formed an ideal location for shipbuilding and the great reserves of coal and iron so necessary to power the industrial revolution were predominantly located in the north. Political events such as the American Civil War in the 1860s, with the consequent demand for fast ships to beat the federal blockade of southern ports, also encouraged experimentation and technical development. This growing concentration of industrial and shipbuilding strength inevitably resulted in a comparable decline on the Thames and in the south generally. The unfortunate saga of the construction of Brunel's massive *Great Eastern* on the Thames at Millwall between 1854 and 1858, with all its mishaps and delays, can perhaps be seen symbolically as a doomed final attempt to compete with the growing giants of Scotland and the north of England, although the Thames Ironworks managed to continue to build large warships until 1911. For by the last years of the nineteenth century major shipbuilding activity (apart from the royal dockyards) was largely restricted to the banks of the northern rivers and estuaries. While a number of shipbuilders such as Thornycroft's maintained profitable and productive yards,

these southern firms tended to specialize in smaller craft. Alongside the yards of Clydeside, it was from the slips of Cammell Laird's at Birkenhead, Vickers-Armstrong at Barrow and Harland and Wolff at Belfast (among a host of other less legendary names) that the great iron and steel liners and cargo steamers were launched. A high proportion of the world's shipping in the last decades of the century was produced from the yards of Tyneside. Charles Palmer's yard at Jarrow had built its first steam collier, the *John Bowes*, in 1852 and its immediate commercial success, together with the impetus to warship construction supplied by the Crimean War, established Tyneside as a leading builder of steam warships. Here in the late nineteenth and early twentieth centuries were built many of the ships of the navies of Japan, Russia, Turkey, Italy and the South American republics. And here was developed the turbine engine which was to provide yet another leap forward in ship construction.

The massive growth in shipbuilding in the nineteenth century was both a response and a stimulus to a new age of travel. Huge movements of people in search of economic opportunity during the course of the century created an expanding mass market for shipping companies, while for the wealthy, by the end of the century luxurious floating hotels made their majestic way back and forth across the Atlantic, as furious competition between companies to produce the fastest and most elegantly appointed vessel inaugurated an age of luxury travel. In no more than sixty years, the British Empire between 1850 and 1911 grew from 4.5 million square miles and a population of 160 million, to 11.5 million square miles and a population of 420 million: this in its turn encouraged the creation of new shipping lines to service these imperial outposts.

Competition for these lucrative markets was intense and both French and German companies built up service networks to challenge British operators. The Compagnie des Services Maritimes des Messageries Impériales expanded out from its Mediterranean base in 1862 with the introduction of an eastern service, while from 1856 the German Hamburg-Amerika Linie concentrated its energies on the North Atlantic. In common with the Bremen-based Norddeutscher Lloyd, which inaugurated its New York service in 1858, the Hamburg-Amerika Linie took a large proportion of the emigrant trade spurned by many of the early British steamship companies. Norddeutscher Lloyd services to the West Indies and South America were introduced in the 1870s, and in the course of the next decade the company was also operating in Australasia and the Far East.

This competition on the ocean routes, particularly from the 1870s, naturally led to improvements in the amenities offered to passengers and the hazardous, cramped and uncomfortable journeys which were the norm for travellers in the early years of the century were gradually replaced by the provision of a relatively comfortable environment. From the early 1880s electric lighting started to replace the smelly and dangerous oil lamps and candles which had previously supplied cabin lighting, while the last years of the century were to see a greatly expanded use of electricity for passenger comfort in the form of heating and ventilating fans and the introduction of refrigerated stores. National pride as well as economic factors was also involved in this competition, and the most hotly contested routes turned into racetracks as speed became the most tangible indicator of superiority. By 1872 the record for a westbound crossing of the Atlantic from Queenstown to New York had been brought down to seven days and twenty-three hours by the White Star Line's *Adriatic*, built by Harland and Wolff; while the following year the Union Line's *Danube* made a record-breaking voyage by covering the 6,000 miles between Southampton and Cape Town in twenty-five and a half days. Four years later, in 1877, this had been further reduced by the Union Line steamer *German*, which completed her passage from Plymouth to the Cape in less than nineteen and a half days, and by 1891 this obsession with speed had brought the record passage time down to under fifteen and a half days.

The twentieth century saw a further leap forward for the great liners. The introduction of steam turbine machinery (first demonstrated at Queen Victoria's Jubilee Review in 1897) in the first years of the new century made for further advances in speed and comfort, and new standards of size and luxury were attained with the launching of Cunard's *Lusitania* at Clydebank in June 1906. At over 30,000 gross tons she was the largest ship in the world, with provision for over 1,200 passengers. Her first-class public rooms achieved an unprecedented elegance of design, and with her sister ship *Mauretania* (Kipling's 'monstrous nine-decked city'), built on the Tyne and launched in the same year, she ushered in a new age of splendour and comfort. Other vessels of similar pretensions followed, each gaining in size and lavishness from her predecessors and competitors. Further heights of elegance were reached with the three White Star giants built by Harland and Wolff at Belfast, the *Olympic*, *Titanic* and *Britannic*. The tragic fate of the *Titanic* is only too well known, while the *Britannic* became a hospital ship straight from the builders and was destined to be an early

victim of the First World War. Only the *Olympic*, delivered for the Southampton to New York run in 1911, saw extensive service. Taking over the mantle of the world's largest ship, she was able to carry a total of nearly 2,400 passengers and surpassed all her contemporaries in the magnificence of her public rooms and first-class facilities, which included squash courts, swimming pools and Turkish baths.

On the outbreak of the First World War in 1914 the passenger liner had perhaps attained its most highly developed form, and major changes were confined to vessels of greater and greater size. The liners of the inter-war years, such as the *Queen Mary*, which in 1936 superseded the ageing *Mauretania* and *Berengeria*, continued this trend, but another war and the post-war growth of mass air travel were ultimately to signal the end of the great liner era.

While the demands of an international trading nation have left their own monuments dominating the industrial landscape of the ports of Great Britain – in the forms of docks, quaysides, warehouses and all the paraphernalia of industrial architecture – a less dramatic maritime tradition, more local, but just as pervasive, has shaped the life of many thousands of seafaring folk. Whether engaged in fishing or in coastal trading, on the open sea or along rivers and inland waterways, there evolved in the different regions of Britain a variety of sailing craft all displaying particular characteristics directly related to their function and the particular topographical peculiarities of the areas from which they originated. The sailing barges, workhorses of coastal and river trade, while all sharing attributes related to their common trade – the shifting of high bulk cargoes such as brick and cement, timber and stone – also evolved distinctive local variations which to the knowledgeable eye immediately betray their place of origin. Most celebrated, and instantly recognizable, is the spritsail barge of the Thames and Medway, descendant of the old river lighters and one of the last survivors of all the seagoing commercial sailing vessels in this country. Massively built yet gracefully proportioned, these craft, with their russet sails and characteristic leeboards and 'sprit', were ideally suited to their trade. Relatively cheap to build, they were also manoeuvrable vessels and a spritsail barge loaded with over 150 tons of cargo could be sailed by a crew of two. Varying in size and type from 40 to 90 feet in length, the largest of them traded as far along the coast as Exeter in the south-west and Hull in the north-east. With the growth of London in the latter half of the nineteenth century, hundreds of these craft were to be seen, laden to within a few inches of freeboard, carrying hay, sand, cement and a thousand other commodities into the greedy mouth of the metropolis. Variations in rig and size – 'stumpie', 'mulie' and 'boomie' are the evocative names of some of the most important varieties of the barges of south-east England – gave these boats an adaptability that enabled the spritsail barge to continue as a working boat into the 1960s.

Further afield, in East Anglia, a characteristic sight along the waterways of the Broads was the great black sail of the Norfolk wherry, a shallow-draft vessel which up to the 1930s shifted cargoes between Norwich and the harbours of Yarmouth and Lowestoft. In the west the sailing barges of Devon and Cornwall traded along the coast and up rivers such as the Tamar, taking their cargoes far inland. Here the barges were divided by rig and build into two classes, 'outside' and 'inside', according to whether they ventured outside sheltered waters. Dozens more of these regional vessel types – the Severn trow with its distinctive square transom stern, the Mersey flat, Humber keels and sloops – moved goods between the coastal and riverine towns and ports of England, performing in a quiet way an economic and social service quite as vital as that of the great cargo vessels of international trade.

But if much of Britain's relationship with the sea has been one of individual struggle and hardship (if also of rich reward to a few), and the unending task of wresting a dangerous living from a volatile and capricious neighbour, on a lighter level this intimate relationship is also seen in the use of the sea for leisure. Despite cheap and easy foreign travel, the lure of the seaside still exerts a powerful pull on the English mind, and historically the seaside holiday was an English invention and later an English export.

Before the eighteenth century the idea of swimming in the sea for pleasure would have been regarded as at best eccentric, at worst immoral, and while swimming was considered a suitably manly accomplishment, this was for the purely pragmatic advantage of possessing a useful skill in times of peril. But England was liberally endowed with spas, and taking the waters had become a fashionable pursuit in the eighteenth century. By asserting the medicinal properties of sea bathing, something of the social cachet of the spa was transferred to the seaside. The town of Scarborough was the first to undergo the metamorphosis from fishing village to fashionable resort, and by the 1730s it was attracting a large summer population eager to frolic in the sea. The pleasures of the seaside, like those of the spas, were disguised as serious therapeutic exercise and generations of quack physicians made a healthy living administering the latest fads to gullible cus-

tomers. While a bracing climate and the pursuit of health were ostensible reasons for the seaside boom, there was always – and continues to be – an agreeably risqué air about the seaside holiday, an excuse for flirtations and frivolity which was early recognized and memorably excoriated by the Reverend John Styles in his tirade against those vices that had led to the fall of 'many young persons now lost to society, [who] have to attribute their ruin to a career of novel reading begun at a watering place'.

The more clement climate of the south coast, accessibility to London and the royal patronage of such resorts as Brighton and Weymouth swiftly led to the transformation of small fishing ports in the late eighteenth century. Formerly insignificant and decaying fishing villages found their seafronts growing by the addition of grandiose stuccoed terraces, while whole new towns came into being to cater for the increased demand for accommodation at places like Bognor and Bournemouth, St Leonard's and Blackpool. But increased demand inevitably signalled a dilution of exclusiveness, and mass-appeal drove the more fashionable classes to the continental resorts. As paid holidays started to be introduced, and cheap transport made such trips possible, the seaside became a popular outing for working-class families. As the century progressed, more mass-market facilities became available: amusement parks and concert halls, Punch and Judy shows and donkey rides on the beach, culminating in the Edwardian heyday in its most characteristic emblem, the seaside pier. Such attractions continue to this day, and the lure of exotic travel has never wholly succeeded in dampening the British enthusiasm for the bracing, wholesome pleasures of the sea air.

Britain's decline as a maritime nation has been steep in recent years. Her share of international shipping tonnage has fallen as a result both of general economic trends and of the increasing use of flags of convenience for ship registration. In addition, the economics of scale introduced by containerization have further diminished that proportion of the population whose living was formerly directly connected to the movement of goods by sea. Many of the great shipbuilding yards have fallen silent in the face of competition from the Far East, while overfishing, diminishing catches and restrictive legislation have all played their part in driving men from the fishing grounds. This country no longer has the imperial possessions nor the pretensions required to justify a naval force equal to or greater than that of any other nation, while the pace of the modern world and the economics of air travel have destroyed the market for the civilized and stately travelling experience on board the great liners.

The majority of the photographs reproduced here look back to that period of a more intense and direct relationship with the sea. Through them we can capture something of the feel of a time when the surrounding sea permeated every level of national life, from the humblest fishing community to the imperial might of the dreadnought battleship. While much of this direct connection with the sea might now have disappeared, photographs, with their penetrating and vivid directness, create a link of unparalleled immediacy with that past, illuminating and enlivening the historical process by which we have become what we are and showing something of what has been gained and lost in the process.

Rotherhithe children, *c.* **1923**

Photograph by William McG. Eager

Little is known of the personal life of this photographer beyond the fact that between 1914 and the early 1920s he lived in Rotherhithe and during this period produced a series of studies of Thameside life. Set against the backdrop of a stark cityscape of riverside ware- houses, these 'water babies' still evoke an age of more innocent amusements. Eager produced a number of photographs of children at play beside the river, pictures in many ways reminiscent in feel- ing of the work of Frank M. Sutcliffe of Whitby.

Above: Old Hungerford Bridge, London, *c.* 1845
Photograph by William Henry Fox Talbot
This view of the old Hungerford Bridge, designed by Isambard Kingdom Brunel and built between 1841 and 1845, was photo-graphed by Fox Talbot very shortly after its completion. The suspension bridge was intended for foot passengers only, and it survived for less than two decades before being replaced by a less attractive railway bridge which was completed in 1864.

The Thames at Wapping, 1860s
Photographer unknown
The schooner *Express* is seen here at her berth at Black Eagle Wharf in the Pool of London at Wapping, surrounded by barges and lighters grounded in the mud. The wharf was situated a little upstream from the original entrance to London Docks.

Left: **Demolishing a dry dock at Limehouse, 1898**
Photographer unknown
The East Indiaman *Canton* was built in 1790, and at the end of her sailing career in 1829 her hull was put to use to form a dry dock at Limehouse. Her astonishingly well-preserved timbers were still firmly in place when workmen demolished the dock seventy years later.

Left: **The Edwards family, dock keepers at Falcon Dock, 1923**
Photograph by William McG. Eager
Many of Eager's photographs vividly capture working-class life among the riverside communities of East London. This portrait of the Edwards family, formally posed at Falcon Wharf at Bankside, is among his most striking images.

Poplar, 13 July 1932
Photographer unknown
This panorama looks across Poplar Docks, towards the *Swift* at her moorings at the east end of the docks. These docks, established in 1852 and extended in 1875, are situated between the West and East India Docks on the Isle of Dogs and at this period formed the goods terminus of the London, Midland and Scottish Railway, whose warehouse can be seen to left of centre in this view.

The Lower Pool, London, *c.* 1923

Photograph by William McG. Eager

Eager's photograph looks westwards along the Thames towards Tower Bridge, with spritsail barges taking the ground on the Rotherhithe shore in the foreground. Until river traffic abandoned the Thames, the Pool, which stretched from Tower Bridge round to the Regent's Canal Dock, was one of the busiest stretches of water on the river. This commercial hub of London was compared by Emile Zola in 1899 to 'an immense moving street of ships, large and small'.

Above: **The barge *Eight Brothers*, 1894**

Photographer unknown

Built at Chiswick in 1894 and owned by S. C. Pearce, the barge is seen here with the eight Pearce brothers after whom she was named. Despite sinking at Gravesend Reach in the following year, she was raised and continued as a working vessel until 1935.

Below: **Thames barges at Surbiton, *c.* 1900**

Photograph by Francis Frith and Co.

Two spritsail barges, the *Glasgow* (built in 1896) and the *James & Ann* (1862), are discharging a cargo of coal or coke at the landing stage opposite Messenger's Boatyard at Surbiton. The *Glasgow* vividly illustrates the low freeboard of a full-laden barge.

Above: **The River Thames frozen at Gravesend, February 1895**

Photograph by Gould and Co.

The winter of 1894–5 was one of historic severity in Great Britain, and not only the Thames but other great rivers such as the Mersey were frozen for several weeks. This photograph was taken as the thaw was beginning. While the river was not frozen solid to any great depth at Gravesend, the *Illustrated London News* reported that at Kingston it was 'so thoroughly frozen that numbers of persons had the memorable experience of crossing the Thames on foot'.

Right: **The River Thames flooded at Gravesend, spring tide, 28 November 1895**

Photograph by Gould and Co.

Weather conditions proved equally severe later in the same year, as this view of a particularly high spring tide illustrates.

Above: **The mission tender *St Andrew* at Gravesend,** *c.* 1905
Photograph by Gould and Co.

The St Andrew's Waterside Mission Church was founded at Gravesend in 1864 by the Reverend C. E. R. Robinson, the incumbent of the parish of Holy Trinity, Milton-next-Gravesend, to minister both to outgoing ships and to the population of the town. A church on the wharfside was completed in 1871 and in later years the mission's activities were extended to other ports. The mission obtained its first small steamer, the *Kestrel*, in 1889. This was replaced by the *St Andrew*, the tender seen here, in 1903. The St Andrew's Mission merged with the Missions to Seamen in 1939.

**Loading the *Clan MacDougall* with frozen meat,
London, April 1938**

Photographer unknown

At the time of this photograph over 100,000 men were employed by the Port of London in the myriad tasks involved in loading and discharging cargoes in the busy docks. Far from being simple labouring, this hard and often dangerous work called upon a variety of skills, and the docks supported a complex network of specialized trades both on board ship, and ashore on the quays and in the warehouses. The 6,843 ton steamer *Clan MacDougall* was built in 1929 and survived until she was torpedoed in 1941.

**Loading the Dutch coastal motor boat *TM 4* on board
the SS *Enggano*, London, 15 January 1929**
Photographer unknown
This photograph shows the *TM 4*, a coastal motor boat built by
Thornycroft for the Dutch Navy in the Far East, being loaded on
board the Dutch-owned cargo steamer *Enggano* (built 1920). She
sailed for Surabaya the following day.

Horstead Mill on the River Bure, East Anglia, *c.* **1902**
Photograph by Francis Frith and Co.
The Norfolk wherry *Widgeon* is seen moored in front of Horstead Mill on the Bure. The only surviving wherries in East Anglia today are pleasure craft, but up until the early 1930s these shallow draught boats with their characteristic great black square sails were a common sight carrying cargoes on the waterways linking Norwich and the ports of Yarmouth and Lowestoft. Horstead Mill was destroyed by fire in 1968.

Opposite: **Folkestone, 1912**
Photograph by Francis Frith and Co.
These tall timber-framed buildings, used for drying nets, were a characteristic sight in many fishing ports of south-east England. This view shows fish merchants' premises in The Stade, near the harbour in Folkestone. This area was redeveloped in the 1920s and 30s and examples of this vernacular architectural style are no longer to be found in the town.

Whitby Harbour, 1890s

Photograph by Frank M. Sutcliffe

Whitby's maritime heritage extends back through the centuries; it was here that Captain Cook started his nautical career on board the colliers that sailed from the port, and Whitby was also a major whaling centre in the eighteenth and nineteenth centuries. It is therefore fitting that the most celebrated of maritime photographers, Frank M. Sutcliffe, should have concentrated almost exclusively on Whitby in his work. This view of the harbour also shows a number of the characteristic local cobles at their moorings.

Opposite above: **Grange-over-Sands, Morecambe Bay, c. 1914**

Photograph by Francis Frith and Co.

Holidaymakers play on the great expanse of sands at Morecambe Bay in this idyllic pre-war scene. Dried out on the beach are two Morecambe Bay prawners or 'nobbies'. These boats, with their yacht-like lines, were designed for working nimbly among the sandbanks and shallow channels of Morecambe Bay as they trawled for prawns; when not out prawning they were sometimes used for pleasure trips in the bay.

Opposite below: **Castle at Lochranza, Arran, 1880s**

Photograph by James Valentine

Isolated island communities in the nineteenth century were dependent on the sea both for their livelihood and for the supply of necessities from the mainland. This view of the picturesque harbour and castle at Lochranza on the north coast of the Isle of Arran shows the boats that serviced both these requirements. In the foreground are fishing smacks (registered at Ardrossan on the mainland), while grounded on the foreshore beyond is a small two-masted schooner engaged in coastal trading.

CASTLE AND LOCHRANZA, ARRAN. 1287. J.V.

Excursion steamer at Bideford, 1880s

Photographer unknown

By the second half of the nineteenth century, pleasure trips were a well-established form of seaside recreation, and the paddle tug *Privateer* is here seen picking up passengers from the quayside in front of the Steam Packet and Railway Hotel at Bideford. *Privateer* was built in 1883 and worked as a tug at Swansea until the mid 1890s; during the summer months she also took holidaymakers across the Bristol Channel from Bideford to Tenby in South Wales.

Left: Holidaymakers at Scarborough, *c.* 1910
Photographer unknown
This charming view by an anonymous amateur photographer was taken at the height of Scarborough's Edwardian popularity, and shows holidaymakers being taken out to a boat for a pleasure trip.

Below: The Grand Parade at Eastbourne, 1870s
Photographer unknown
Although Eastbourne had enjoyed modest popularity as a bathing resort from the late eighteenth century, it was something of a late developer among the south coast seaside resorts. But from 1850, when the population stood at about 3,500, its growth was swift. By the 1880s the population had increased sevenfold, an impressive terrace of stuccoed façades lined the beach and, most important of all, a pier had been built. Work began on the pier in 1866 and the first section was opened in 1870, although it was not until 1888 that a theatre was built on the pierhead.

Mevagissey, *c.* 1890
Photographer unknown
Mevagissey 'toshers' (the open-decked fishing boats in the foreground) and other vessels employed in drift net and line fishing are seen dried out in the busy inner harbour at Mevagissey. As well as fishing boats, other coastal trading vessels came into the port to discharge their cargoes, and in this view the two-masted schooner *Marshal Keith*, built at Peterhead in 1864, can be seen lying at her moorings.

***Opposite:* Street in old St Ives, *c.* 1906**
Photograph by Francis Frith and Co.
Now largely overrun by tourists, St Ives possesses one of the few harbours on the north Cornish coast and at the time of this photograph was a thriving fishing port, with about 200 boats registered in the town. Fish landed at St Ives were taken overland by pack pony to be sold in the thriving market at Mounts Bay, on the south coast of Cornwall.

Opposite: Minehead, c. 1900

Photograph by Francis Frith and Co.

At the period of this photograph Minehead still supported a small fishing fleet, although by the turn of the century this was becoming an increasingly precarious way of earning a living as the appearance of the herring shoals became more erratic and unpredictable. Already Minehead was starting to develop as a holiday centre and, like St Ives and many other small harbours along this coast, tourism now forms its economic mainstay.

Above: Fisher folk, Llangwm, Pembrokeshire, c. 1906

Photograph by Francis Frith and Co.

Below: Lympstone, c. 1896

Photograph by Francis Frith and Co.

Situated on the east bank of the Exe estuary a few miles south-east of Exeter, Lympstone was a thriving fishing village at this period, as the nets and lines hanging on the foreshore testify. The village also benefited from the rich oyster beds planted in the area.

Top: **Royal Pier, Southampton, 1870s**
Photographer unknown
A steam packet service between Southampton and Cowes had been in operation since 1820, and this view shows the mainland terminus, Royal Pier (built in 1833), with the offices of the Southampton, Isle of Wight & South of England Royal Mail Steam Packet Company, in the foreground.

Bottom: **Clacton Pier, c. 1904**
Photograph by Francis Frith and Co.
Developed as a rival to Margate for the London day-tripper trade, this quiet Essex fishing village was transformed into a bustling sea-side resort in the second half of the nineteenth century. The old village pier was replaced by this structure in 1872, and by 1887 over 25,000 trippers a year were taking the steamer to Clacton.

Opposite above: **St George's landing stage, Liverpool, 1890s**
Photographer unknown
This photograph shows part of the floating landing stage which was the boarding point for ferries and ocean-going vessels. It appears to have been taken at midday, when, according to the *Liverpool Review*, 'the number of city men, clerks and apprentices who stroll the length of the stage during the dinner hour is very considerable . . . Many men, from the seedy greasy loafer to the city merchant, take a delight in seeing the coasting boats arrive and depart and the tenders leave for the ocean greyhounds lying in the river.'

Opposite below: **Graving Docks at Liverpool, c. 1890**
Photographer unknown
The building of the Langton Graving Dock was authorized by Act of Parliament in 1873 and construction was completed in 1879. Opened for the specific purpose of accommodating the largest vessels in the North Atlantic service, it failed to make provision for the increasing size of ships and was already inadequate by the late 1880s. The steamship seen on the right is the *Frank Pendleton*.

Above: The *Great Britain*, c. 1844
Photographer unknown
This view of Brunel's *Great Britain* moored at Bristol is one of the earliest surviving photographic images of a steamship.

Opposite: Foundry workers, Thames Ironworks, 1880s
Photographer unknown
Situated at the mouth of Bow Creek, Thames Ironworks was the most important shipbuilding firm on the river from the mid nineteenth century until its demise in 1912. During this period 144 warships and 287 merchant ships were built for both domestic and foreign customers, and it was from this yard that HMS *Warrior*, then the largest warship in the world, was launched in 1860. Half a century later, in 1911, the 22,000 ton HMS *Thunderer* was launched from the yard, the last battleship to be built on the Thames.

Below: The *Great Eastern* under construction at Millwall, 18 August 1855
Photograph by Joseph Cundall
This view shows the monumental central section of the 'monster ship' (as the *Illustrated London News* referred to her), before the hull was plated up. Laid down in 1854 and launched in 1858, this revolutionary vessel was, at nearly 19,000 tons, the largest ship afloat.

**Carpentry shop at the John Brown Shipyard,
Clydebank, 1901**

Photograph by Bedford Lemère

The famous firm of John Brown originated in the marine engineering business founded in 1847 by James and George Thomson. In 1851 they opened a shipyard at Cessnock Bank, Govan, and their first vessel, the paddle steamer *Jackal*, was launched the following year. But it was the move to Dalmuir on Clydebank in 1871 and the opening of a large modern engine works in 1884 that allowed the company to become one of the greatest shipbuilding firms in the country. The firm passed out of family hands as a result of the depression of 1897 and was taken over by the Sheffield steelmakers John Brown in 1899.

The launch of the Cunard liner *Aquitania*, Clydebank, 21 April 1913

Photograph by Bedford Lemère

The early years of the twentieth century saw intense rivalry between shipping companies for the lucrative North Atlantic express service. The *Aquitania*, and her partners on the service *Lusitania* and *Mauretania*, were designed to compete in particular against the White Star Line's *Olympic*, launched in 1910. This *Aquitania* was well placed to do, and with a length of 900 feet and a gross tonnage of nearly 47,000 tons, she was the largest ship in the world, surpassing anything previously seen on the North Atlantic route. Her construction was followed with tremendous public interest, from the laying of her first keel plate on 5 June 1911 to her launch two years later.

***Above:* Captain W. T. Turner, Master of the *Aquitania*, 1913**

Photograph by Bedford Lemère

The *Aquitania*'s first captain is seen here posed formally in the full dress uniform of a captain of the Royal Naval Volunteer Reserve. *Aquitania* was to have a distinguished career of thirty-five years that spanned two world wars (in which she served variously as armed merchant cruiser, hospital ship and troop carrier) before she was finally sold for scrap in 1950.

Below: **The liner *Scot* in the Denny Shipyard, Dumbarton,** *c.* **1890**
Photographer unknown

The Denny family had been involved in shipbuilding since the first quarter of the nineteenth century, but the firm became most solidly established as a result of the shipbuilding boom at the time of the American Civil War. One of their major specialities was the construction of shallow draught steamers for tropical rivers, and until the firm's liquidation in 1963 they were also the leading builders of cross-Channel steamers. The *Scot*, completed in 1891, was designed for speed and on her maiden voyage reached Cape Town in a record time of fifteen days. She was broken up in 1927.

Opposite above: Haverford **being fitted out at the John Brown Shipyard, Clydebank, 1901**
Photograph by Bedford Lemère

This view of the yard was taken shortly after it had been taken over by John Brown & Co. A modernization programme was immediately put in hand to install the plant and other facilities that allowed the yard to compete for big Admiralty and merchant shipping contracts. Between this time and the firm's takeover by Upper Clyde Shipbuilders in 1968, many famous vessels were launched from here, including the *Lusitania* (1913), HMS *Hood* (1920), the *Queen Mary* (1934), the *Queen Elizabeth* (1938) and the *QEII* (1967).

Opposite below: **Thames Ironworks, London, 1880s**
Photographer unknown

In 1863 the writer P. Barry included a chapter on this shipyard in his *Dockyard Economy and Naval Power*. He reserved particular praise for the efficiency of the machinery and for the layout of the yard, contrasting it favourably to the situation in Royal Naval establishments, where, he claimed, little thought was given to the overall design of working areas. The yard was also well located near the railway and, again according to Barry, was capable of handling 25,000 tons of ironclad warships and 10,000 tons of merchant shipping simultaneously.

John Thornycroft with his first boat, the steam launch *Nautilus*, 1862
Photographer unknown

Carpet-making shop at the John Thornycroft Shipyard, Woolston, Southampton, 1921
Photographer unknown

Opposite below: **Foundry at the John Thornycroft Shipyard, Woolston, Southampton, *c.* 1912**
Photographer unknown

Sir John Isaacs Thornycroft (1843–1928) served a period as a draughtsman with Palmer's Shipyard at Jarrow before opening his own yard on the Thames at Chiswick in 1866. The firm specialized in small craft, particularly torpedo boats, but when they started to build larger destroyers in the 1890s, the obstacle of Hammersmith Bridge became a major inconvenience and in 1906 Thornycrofts moved to a new yard at Woolston near Southampton. A boatyard was also maintained in Singapore during the 1920s, and in 1929 an additional yard was opened at Northam. The firm remains in business today under the name Vosper Thornycroft.

Coaling the *Balantia* at St Lucia, 23 November 1911

Photographer unknown

The Royal Mail Steam Packet Company won its first contract for the delivery of mails to the West Indies in 1840, and in subsequent years built up an inter-island network of deliveries and passenger services based on Barbados. The *Balantia*, built by Harland and Wolff in 1909, worked this inter-island route and is here seen being coaled at the company depot on St Lucia. *Balantia* later served as a hospital ship in the First World War and was broken up in 1929.

Firemen at work, *c.* **1900**

Photographer unknown

Photographs of the men known as firemen in the merchant service and stokers in the Royal Navy are rare, but they performed a vital, if largely invisible, role in the life of the steamship. Their job was as dangerous as any on board ship, with the additional discomforts of fearsome heat, confined working conditions, lack of ventilation and the health hazards of constant exposure to coal dust and gases.

Funnels of the *Aquitania*, 1914

Photograph by Bedford Lemère

Above: Emigrants leaving Southampton, *c.* **1910**
Photographer unknown

Although the nineteenth century saw huge advances in passenger transport across the Atlantic, most shipping firms showed little initial interest in the emigrant traffic, preferring to compete with their rivals at the luxury end of the market. Better conditions for poorer travellers inevitably percolated down, however, and by the time of this photograph such travellers were at least assured reasonable if somewhat spartan accommodation.

Below: Afternoon leisure on the SS *Orizaba*, *c.* **1888**
Photographer unknown

The *Orizaba*, built for the Pacific Steam Navigation Company in 1886, was one of the first of the company's ships to use the Suez Canal on both the outward and return legs of the Australian run. She was employed on this route until 1905, when she was stranded and sunk off Fremantle. The *Orient Line Guide* of 1890 assured the prospective traveller on the *Orizaba* that no effort or expense had been spared for the comfort of its passengers.

Opposite above: **First class dining room on the *Omrah*, c. 1899**
Photograph by Bedford Lemère
The steady improvement in passenger facilities had reached a peak of luxury by the end of the century as the shipping lines competed

to make their vessels ever more elegant and attractive. Built for the Orient Line's Australian service, the 8,000 ton steamer *Omrah* boasted a first class dining room of overpowering and claustrophobic pretension, festooned with a bizarre extravagance of architectural motifs.

Opposite below: **Third class dining room on the *Saxonia*, c. 1900**
Photograph by Bedford Lemère
While the opulence of first class accommodation figured most prominently in the publicity for the great liners, by the end of the century this accounted for only a small proportion of their passengers. The *Saxonia*, built on the Clyde in 1900 for Cunard's Atlantic service, had accommodation for a mere 164 first and 200 second class passengers, while the area of the main deck forward of the engine room was designed to carry 1,500 third class passengers in more basic conditions. In fact, these passengers realized much greater profits and both *Saxonia* and her sister ship *Invernia* were later diverted to the route taking mainly Italian and Hungarian emigrants from the Mediterranean to America.

Above: **Barber's shop on the *Olympic*, c. 1912**
Photograph by Bedford Lemère
The magnificent White Star liner *Olympic* was the largest ship in the world when she was launched in 1910, although she was soon overtaken by her sisters *Titanic* and *Britannic*. Her career started inauspiciously when at the start of her first voyage she was involved in a collision with HMS *Hawke* off Southampton. However, she played a distinguished role as a troop transport during the First World War, carrying over 200,000 men, and was not finally broken up until 1937.

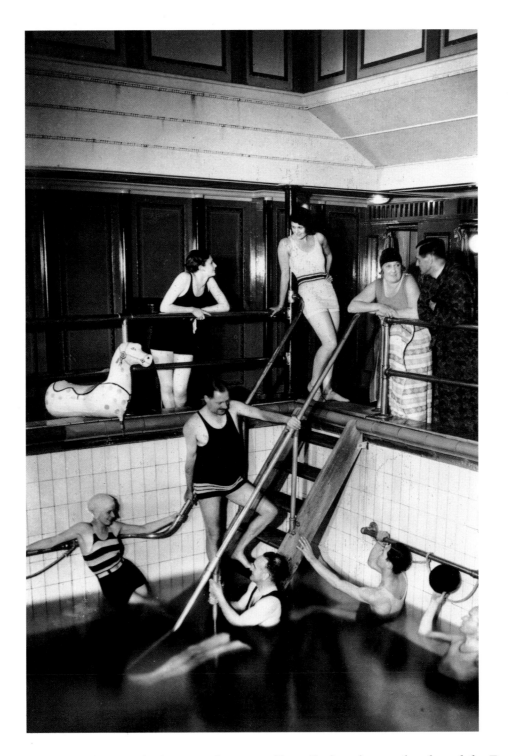

Opposite: First class smoking room (*above*) and winter garden (*below*) on the *Empress of Scotland*, 1920s

Photograph by Bedford Lemère

Built in 1905 as the *Kaiserin Auguste Victoria*, this liner was one of the most popular vessels on the North Atlantic run and was renowned for the luxuriousness of her fittings. She was purchased by Canadian Pacific in 1921 and in 1927 was chosen to take the Prince of Wales back to England after his Canadian tour. By the end of her career in 1930 she had completed seventy-one Atlantic voyages.

Above: Swimming pool on board the *Empress of Australia*, c. 1930

Photographer unknown

Like the *Empress of Scotland*, the *Empress of Australia* was a German-built ship taken over at the end of the war as reparation. Built in 1913 as the *Tirpitz*, she was acquired by Canadian Pacific for their North Atlantic service in 1927. This photograph is one of a series of very posed views taken on board a number of Canadian Pacific liners for advertising purposes.

THE HARVEST OF THE SEA

Mackerel drivers leaving Penzance, *c.* 1886
Photograph by Gibson of Penzance

As European community quotas step in to regulate the depleted fish stocks in the waters around the British coast, it is hard to appreciate the wealth of marine life around these islands, a resource which for hundreds of years has formed both a staple item of diet and a profitable source of export income. The coming of the age of photography coincided with the height of the fishing boom in Britain as technology and demand conspired to exploit the harvest of the sea, and images of the busy life of Britain's fishing harbours supply vivid testimony to a phenomenon which in the last years of the century made the Scottish industry the greatest in the world. The very busyness of these scenes, however,

Scottish fifies in harbour, *c.* 1910

Photographer unknown

The fifie was the dominant type of fishing boat on the east coast of Scotland between Eyemouth and Aberdeen. With a length of up to sixty feet and a beam of twenty feet, it was among the most powerful lugsailed craft of the British Isles. Until the mid nineteenth century fifies were entirely open, but they were later built with decks. As their size increased they roamed further afield in search of fish, and a few boats were even owned as far south as Yarmouth and Lowestoft. By negotiating the locks of the Caledonian Canal, these adaptable boats were also able to fish the waters of the Irish Sea. Although a few were later adapted for use with auxiliary engines, the changed conditions of the herring industry after the First World War spelled the end for these sturdy boats.

was itself an unheeded warning of the success with which a developing maritime technology could comb the sea and ultimately denude it of its riches.

While the position today is more critical than ever, such conservation concerns are not new. The dangers of overfishing were well appreciated by our ancestors, and as long ago as 1376 a petition was presented to Parliament protesting against the use of the recently introduced beam trawl which, it was argued, caught undersized fish and damaged and bruised much of the catch: for 'the great and long iron of the wondrychoun [as the new trawl was called] runs so heavily and hardily over the ground . . . that it destroys the flowers of the land below the water'. In succeeding centuries restrictive or protective legislation was from time to time enacted, but it is perhaps only when we compare photographs of the bustling and crowded harbours of the nineteenth and early twentieth centuries with their depressed counterparts today that we fully appreciate the wealth that has been dissipated. The introduction of the steam trawler and drifter and their ever more efficient progeny, together with increasingly effective methods of fish detection, have all played their part in turning 'the land below the water' into a desert. It is hard now for us to comprehend the astonishing and seemingly limitless richness of the sea, a glorious harvest that astonished our ancestors and persisted into the early years of the present century.

English fishermen had ventured out into the North Atlantic to seek the great shoals of cod since medieval times, and the catch, salted and dried, was brought home for use particularly during Lent when the eating of meat was forbidden. Icelandic waters were the first fishing grounds of the slow and lumbering vessels which ventured out from these shores to bring back the 'beef of the sea'. Ketch-rigged English boats called 'doggers' sailed north in the spring and spent the season fishing for cod on handlines. Salting and drying was done on board and at the end of the season the boats returned home with the catch. Regular little fleets sailed from all the major ports of eastern England, the now disappeared town of Dunwich, for instance, sending some twenty ships a year to Iceland during the reign of Edward I. In addition to its economic importance the fishing industry was valued as a pool of skilled seamen that could be drawn upon in time of national emergency: thus Elizabeth I, despite her father's break with Rome, brought back non-flesh-eating days in order to encourage the industry.

By this time English seamen were sailing further afield, to the rich fishing grounds off the foggy eastern seaboard of Canada. Discovered by the Cabots in 1497 during their fruitless search for a new route to the east, the waters off Newfoundland and Labrador held huge quantities of cod and within a few years these seas had attracted the fleets of all the maritime nations of Europe. Until the development of Arctic trawling in the 1890s, these were the prime distant water fishing grounds, although the English, in the face of increasing competition, had largely ceased to fish the Newfoundland Banks by the 1830s and were turning their attention to the waters nearer home.

In northern European waters the herring was the main catch, and records of large-scale herring fishing go back to tenth-century Sweden. But with the decline of the Baltic trade the focus switched to the North Sea, which by the seventeenth century was dominated by the Dutch, who had taken full advantage of the English preference for the Atlantic fishing grounds. By the 1620s the Dutch herring fleet numbered around 2,000 vessels, efficiently organized and renowned for the quality of their cured fish. This dominance was fiercely resented by the English, who, since they could not compete with the quality of the Dutch product, resorted to legislation in an attempt to undermine the Dutch hegemony of the North Sea. Cromwell's Navigation Act of 1651 banned foreign vessels from landing goods at British ports and resulted in the outbreak of the First Anglo-Dutch War of 1652–4. By the end of the Third Anglo-Dutch War in 1674

Dutch maritime power was in decline, although the herring industry continued on a reduced scale up to the nineteenth century. As Dutch power waned, the English became more involved in the North Sea fisheries, and although many early voyages failed through lack of skill in curing and preserving the catch, this was a minor setback to the development of an industry which by the end of the nineteenth century was to supply a dangerous livelihood to many thousands of men and women. From the mid seventeenth century until the development of the railway network, Great Yarmouth (which had been the only port to benefit significantly from the Dutch herring fleet) was the most important east coast fishing port, and by the middle of the last century it was the home port to over 200 fishing luggers sailing to the rich herring grounds which ran parallel to the Norfolk coast.

It was the last half of the nineteenth century and the early years of the present century which saw the British fishing industry at its height, and around the coast distinctive boat types adapted to suit local conditions evolved to accommodate advances in building technology and improved types of fishing gear. While various traditional methods, such as long lining, continued to be used for certain types of fish, two specific methods had achieved overall dominance by the middle of the nineteenth century. They were determined by the nature of the catch. For pelagic or surface-feeding fish such as mackerel, pilchard and herring the drift net was used. These nets, some 30 feet deep and nearly 200 feet long, hung from the surface to trap the fish. Nets would be paid out at sunset, and for the rest of the night the boats would drift with the tide. The back-breaking work of hauling in the nets at dawn was somewhat eased by the introduction of the steam capstan in the late 1870s. Demersal fish such as cod, haddock and sole which live at greater depth or on the bottom of the sea were caught by trawling, a method which essentially drags a sack-shaped net along the seabed, scooping up fish. The two main types of trawl were the beam trawl, by which the mouth of the net was held open by a beam, and the otter trawl. This latter was introduced in the 1870s, and used water pressure against two boards on either side of the net to hold the mouth open.

The Scottish herring fishery also developed as the Dutch declined during the course of the seventeenth century, but it was not until the early nineteenth century that it started to become a successful large-scale industry. This came with the major harbour improvements of the early years of the century and, more importantly, success in producing a herring curing method that rivalled the Dutch. In 1819 the bounty offered by the Royal Society of Arts for a curing method was awarded, and within a few years the crown symbol branded on barrels of Scottish herrings became a byword for quality throughout Europe.

The huge expansion of the herring industry by the middle years of the century is graphically portrayed in photographs of ports like Wick, on Scotland's north-east coast. Fishermen had sailed from Wick from the earliest times and it remains to this day the centre for the Highlands inshore fishing fleet. But the prosperity enjoyed by the town in the mid nineteenth century is now gone: at that period a fifth of Scotland's herring were landed there, and from about 600 boats in the 1820s, the port's home fleet had grown to over 1,000 by the early 1860s. Each summer a 'herring madness' hit the town as men and women flocked to Wick from all over the Highlands for seasonal employment, working on the boats or in the curing yards for the six-week fishing period. This influx brought its own problems, and while photographs of the port show something of the bustle of activity during the season, they cannot hope to evoke more than a fraction of the atmosphere of the 'indescribably filthy' streets, with 'everywhere putrescent effluvia steaming up from the fish offals'. Typhoid too was a constant danger during this period, when the incomers crowded into insanitary lodgings for the course of the season.

While the fishermen faced danger at sea, the lot of their womenfolk was little better – the danger replaced by hardship and tedium, and with little hope of maintaining more than a fragile economic equilibrium. In small Scottish villages it was the women who gathered mussels and other forms of seashore life to bait the lines, they who made and repaired the fisherman's clothes, and they who sold his produce. Before the days of the railway they tramped from door to door selling the catch. They often covered miles carrying heavy baskets of fish, sometimes working in relays, since speed was of the essence and stale fish would find no market. The railways changed this pattern, but introduced a new role for the women of the fishing community. At the same time as the transport of fish to more distant markets became more mechanized, so the boats were growing in size, becoming more seaworthy and allowing the men to follow the herring for most of the year. Setting off from the Shetlands in early summer, the boats sailed south after the migrating shoals, ending up in East Anglia at the end of the year. Behind them came the women, who travelled down in special trains to work at gutting and packing the herring catch. These women worked in crews of three gutting and packing the fish, con-

tinuing late into the night if the catch was large. Their fingers bound in bandages known as 'clooties' to protect themselves against their razor-sharp knives and the rough salt, their clothes covered in fish-guts and scales, they worked at phenomenal speed. Standing in front of a wooden trough known as a 'farlin', two of them gutted while the third packed the fish between layers of salt. Barrels contained about 700 fish, and in the course of a day a crew might pack thirty barrels. In the early years of the century these women were paid eleven shillings a week, with their lodgings and travel thrown in. Despite the harshness of their working conditions the women were renowned for their scrupulous cleanliness and neatness when off-duty, and many looked back on these days with affection and nostalgia for the comradeship of their fellows.

But the larger boats brought their own dangers. At the beginning of the nineteenth century the small fishing boats common on the east coast of Scotland could be easily beached in small coves. By the 1850s boat size had increased to the extent that the ill-maintained harbours were inadequate: boats were commonly up to forty feet long, displacing about five tons and now in need of deep harbours to run to in the event of a sudden storm. The harbour work undertaken at the beginning of the century was inadequate for the number and size of boats and at low tide most of the harbours were inaccessible. In 1848 this lack of planning and maintenance was highlighted by tragedy. On the night of 19 August a huge south-easterly gale blew up as over 900 boats fished off the north-east coast. As the boats ran for shelter, the townspeople of Wick watched impotently as twenty-five men died at the harbour entrance, where raging seas and less than five feet of water prevented them from reaching the safety of the port. A similar story was told at Peterhead, where the already narrow harbour entrance was obstructed by moored steamers. The final toll was 124 boats lost and 100 men dead. The Parliamentary inquiry which followed traced the 'grand cause' of the disaster to the state of the harbours. Additional factors were lack of foresight among the fishermen themselves, as well as the lack of experience of the many landsmen – an average of three out of every five men in the boats were not trained seamen – who were not sufficiently skilled to handle their craft in an emergency. The harbour problem was never satisfactorily resolved, with the result that the Scottish industry on the east coast became concentrated at its peak on the four ports of Buckie, Fraserburgh, Peterhead and Aberdeen.

But central to the problem was why the boats had been

unable to ride out the storm, and in this the innate conservatism of the fishing community was crucial. Scottish fishermen, unlike those in the south and west, insisted on using open boats for herring fishing, arguing, among other reasons, that decked boats were too heavy to row against light winds, and stowing nets in a hold was impractical because they had to be landed and dried daily. And so the use of these unnecessarily dangerous craft continued for a further two decades. An initiative by the National Lifeboat Institution, which built and hired out a number of forty-foot decked boats in 1867, made some impression on the 'inert class' of fishermen, and by the early 1870s an increasing proportion of decked vessels were being built. This led to the development of the most characteristic and elegant of the large Scottish fishing boats of the last quarter of the nineteenth century. As the advantages of the decked boat became more apparent, two local types of boat emerged. On the southern shores of the Moray Firth the 'scaffie', a nimble short-keeled boat with a rounded stem and sharply raked stern, was favoured, while elsewhere on the east coast the 'fifie', a long-keeled boat with vertical stem and stern, became the standard herring drifter pattern. Both types used the dipping lugsail rig, often cumbersome to use, but simple and powerful, and both had their own advantages and disadvantages in terms of speed, stability and manoeuvrability.

It was a combination of the best features of both these types that in 1879 produced the 'zulu', named after the colonial war then raging. Amalgamating the raked stern of the scaffie with the vertical stem of the fifie produced a boat with maximum deck area which retained the sailing characteristics of the fifie. The hardy zulu, with its tree-like sixty-foot mast, represents the zenith of Scottish sailing drifter design, and was adopted by all the fishing ports on the Moray Firth. Massively built yet handsome in their lines, these boats are a characteristic sight in photographs of the last years of the century, a forest of masts in the harbours of the east coast of Scotland.

Remote and economically backward until the coming of the railways in the mid nineteenth century, the fishermen of south-west England developed their own traditions and fishing methods, largely independent of the other fishing grounds. While their fellows on the east coast chased the herring and haddock, the staple quarry of the Cornish fishermen was pilchard and mackerel. And as in each regional area, topography, custom and fishing practice led to the development of characteristic boat types.

The mackerel drifters or 'drivers' of the Cornish coast were descendants of the fast three-masted luggers used on this smugglers' coast to evade the revenue men; in the course of the nineteenth century a further identifiable local characteristic was developed, the product of topography and the characteristics of the harbours of the area. In the more spacious east Cornish harbours, boats with square transom sterns were the norm, but to the west where tiny harbours and coves were more common the boats had pointed sterns to allow as many as possible to be moored together without damage. Many of these sturdy boats stayed working for the best part of a century, and their owners remained faithful to the lug rig and drift net fishing while the ports of Devon developed as trawling centres.

The character of the Cornish industry changed dramatically after 1859 when the railway bridge over the Tamar brought new markets for mackerel and pilchard. Activity became focused on the larger harbours, particularly Newlyn, and bigger boats fished further and further out to sea. But this expansion itself foretold the end of the industry, as east coast drifters and trawlers exhausted the fishing grounds.

It was also in Cornwall that a method unique in this country was employed for catching the pilchard, a method that remained little changed from the sixteenth to the end of the nineteenth centuries. The Cornish seine netting industry relied on the unpredictable arrival of shoals of pilchard, subtropical fish whose northern limits were the south-west coast of England and which from time to time in late summer and early autumn came close inshore where they could be surrounded by seine nets. Lookouts stationed on a cliff-top would alert the fishermen below with cries of 'Hevva! Hevva!' when a shoal of pilchard moved like a shadow across the sea, and in scenes of hectic activity the boats were directed to the shoal by signals from the 'huer' on the cliffs. Their aim was to encircle the entire shoal with nets which would then be dragged close to the shore. Here the net was moored and the fish kept alive until they could be taken ashore for curing. The whole operation was controlled by the master seiner from a boat called the 'lurker', and while the net was drawn round the shoal another boat, known as the 'volyer', or follower, took a net across the mouth of the seine to prevent any fish escaping. Millions of fish might be caught in this way in a few hours, and a seine might take as long as a week to be emptied. From the boats the fish were taken to the curing cellars where they were laid out at great speed between layers of salt. Most of the traditional seining centres were driven out of business by drift net fishing, which disrupted the pattern of the shoals, and by the early years of this century only St Ives continued the tradition. The last catch was made in 1908, although it was not until 1922 that the annual watch for the shoals was finally abandoned.

A little further east in South Devon was Brixham, arguably the home of trawling. Brixham had been a fishing port for hundreds of years, but claims credit for introducing the large beam trawl which was to increase catches hugely. As a growing population increased demand in the first decades of the nineteenth century, Brixham boats moved eastwards to be nearer the London markets; and by the 1820s and 30s Brixham trawlers were competing for the fish of the North Sea, with a fleet of Devon boats even basing itself at Scarborough for the summer. The coming of the big trawlers to the east coast ports signalled the start of a boom which in the long term was to rival that of the Scottish fisheries. The following decades, particularly after the development of the railway network, saw a massive growth in fishing ports such as Hull, Grimsby and Great Yarmouth where, for example, the trawler fleet grew from about a dozen in 1850 to over 400 in 1875. The fleet system, in which one returning boat brought back the fleet's catch and allowed the trawlers to stay out longer, was introduced in the North Sea in the 1850s and increased catches greatly. This was to be a portent of modern fishing methods.

The first trawler was converted to steam in 1877 and signalled a turning point in fishing history. Far larger trawls could be dragged and the boats were no longer dependent on wind and tide. Signs of over-fishing soon became evident and by the 1890s new grounds were being sought. Ironically enough the boats reverted to Icelandic waters in the 1890s, and to the Newfoundland Banks and Greenland in the early years of the present century. Steam came to drift-net fishing boats a little later – the Lowestoft steam drifter *Consolation* was built in 1898 – but with similar results. Equally important were the social effects of this change, which tended to concentrate ownership in company fleets rather than with individuals and led to the breaking up of the fishing communities.

Photographs supply a vivid and evocative picture of these busy ports, the sturdy craft crammed up against each other suggesting economic as well as physical buoyancy. The intervening years have added their own patina of romance to a falsely picturesque view with which the photographers themselves were only too willing to collude. For the sea was always a precarious and dangerous calling, which held little hope of substantial reward for the majority of those directly employed in the fishing trade. The Merchant Shipping Act of 1854 had instituted an apprenticeship system for the fishing industry; for many young boys this long ten years of virtual slavery was their introduction to the sea, and many preferred escape and possible imprisonment to the rigours of life at sea. An indication of the harshness of their life is seen in their response to the Act of 1880 which abolished the power to arrest deserting apprentices without a warrant: hundreds immediately fled the boats, causing a severe crisis in the manning of the fleet at Hull. An apprentice who survived might in his twenties, with skill and ambition, become a skipper in the employment of a fleet owner, but for the majority the fisherman's life was ill-paid, arduous and dangerous. Long weeks of back-breaking toil in heavy, damp and dirty clothes, poor food and cramped accommodation were the norm. The surviving reminiscences of some of these old fishermen paint a harsh picture of life on board the sailing vessels, and few mourned their passing and the advent of steam. A Great Yarmouth smacksman whose reminiscences were recorded in 1909 called it a 'rum, hard life', adding, 'I'd as soon be a conwick as go through it all again.' But in spite of the harsh conditions, the dangers of that 'regular ocean cemetery' the Dogger Bank, and the poor rewards, the craft of the fisherman, for those who survive, is ultimately a heroic endeavour: 'People ought to think well of the smacksman, for his hardihood, let alone for the price paid for the fish they eat, what have often been caught for them at the sacrifice of a fisherman's life.'

WICK HARBOUR. HERRING SEASON. 2110.

Wick Harbour during the herring season, 1880s

Photograph by George Washington Wilson

At this period a fifth of Scotland's herring catch was landed at Wick and over 1,000 drifters sailed from the port. A 'herring madness' – likened to the atmosphere of a frontier gold-rush town – descended on Wick during the frenetic two-month season as men and women tramped across the Highlands in search of employment either on the boats or in the curing yards. Outbreaks of disease, particularly typhoid, were common in the limited accommodation that was available, and the atmosphere of pictures such as this lacks perhaps the most vital component of the scene – the smell of the 'indescribably filthy' streets, with 'everywhere a putrescent effluvia streaming up from the fish offals'.

Herring packers at Scarborough, *c.* **1910**
Photographer unknown
As fishing boats grew more seaworthy, herring could be followed throughout the year, from the Shetlands in May down to East Anglia at Christmas. The fishermen's families also followed the fleets, working in crews of three at the wooden bins known as 'far-lins' where the fish were gutted and salted for packing. To earn a living wage required a high work-rate, and a skilled crew could pack thirty barrels of fish a day – a fish every five seconds through the course of a ten-hour day.

A St Ives pilchard seine, *c.* **1910**
Photographer unknown
The huge shoals of pilchard that swept along the Cornish coast were caught by seine netting, a method that in England dates back to the sixteenth century. Whole shoals were encircled by the seine net, the ends of which would be drawn together to trap the fish. The net was then towed into shallow water where the seine acted as a keep-net for the live fish until they were removed for curing.

Lowestoft lugger running for Penzance, *c.* 1894
Photograph by Gibson of Penzance
Photographs of fishing boats in heavy seas are uncommon, and this dramatic view shows the Lowestoft lugger LT 303 running for Penzance with sail taken in. Many east coast luggers fished as far afield as the West Country, and considering the hard usage they received often had a long life. Several such vessels remained in service for forty or fifty years.

**Mine brought up by the Plymouth trawler *Genesta*
(PH 18), November 1934**

Photographer unknown

Not all the perils of the sea can be laid at nature's door, as this mine brought up by the motor trawler *Genesta* on 22 November 1934 indicates. This British surface mine had been sunk by gunfire at the end of the First World War, but remained live and contained 250 lb of gun cotton when it was trawled from the seabed by *Genesta*. In this instance the only damage sustained was to the trawler's nets, which were torn when the mine was brought on board and required £20 worth of repairs.

Below: **Landing whelks at Wells-next-the-Sea,** *c.* **1929**
Photograph by Francis Frith and Co.
The fishing boom which brought wealth to the big East Anglian
ports of Yarmouth and Lowestoft is now a thing of the past, but
several of the smaller towns along this coast still rely on the sea for
their livelihood. The north Norfolk port of Wells-next-the-Sea still
supplies a large proportion of the whelks eaten in Britain today, in
addition to cockles and crabs.

Right: **Sheringham fishermen,** *c.* **1906**
Photograph by Francis Frith and Co.
Like Wells-next-the-Sea, nearby Sheringham still also maintains a
fleet of small fishing boats, specializing in the catching of crab and
other crustacea that thrive on the offshore banks of sand along the
north Norfolk coast. The heavy leather sea-boots and oiled sou'-
westers worn by these men have nowadays been exchanged for
lighter gear, but the crab boats against which they pose have
remained largely unaltered in design. Although now powered by a
motor rather than a lugsail, these handy little boats are perfectly
adapted for their task and their form has changed little in the course
of a century.

Caulking a Brixham fishing smack, *c.* 1900
Photographer unknown
Wooden sailing vessels required constant work to maintain them in a seaworthy condition, and here the crew of the trawler *Dauntless* (DH 121) are seen forcing new caulking between the boat's timbers with the special tool used for the purpose. *Dauntless*, built at Brixham in 1885, had seen some fifteen years of service when this picture was taken.

Opposite above: **Sail loft at Appledore,** *c.* 1900
Photographer unknown
Making sails for both fishing boats and larger vessels required a large open space for the laying out of canvas, and such work was carried out in the lofts on the upper storeys of a shipyard building. Treadle machines for sewing canvas were introduced in the late nineteenth century, and two can be seen by the windows in this photograph of a small sail loft at Appledore.

Opposite below: **Barking sails at Brixham,** *c.* 1900
Photographer unknown
Before use, the sails of trawlers were dressed or barked to a russet colour with a preservative solution of cutch tanning and tallow. Men are here seen working the solution into the canvas, with treated sails drying in the background.

Drying nets at Stonehaven, *c.* **1897**

Photograph by G. Miller

Although Stonehaven, situated on the east coast of Scotland south of Aberdeen, was a minor curing centre in the late nineteenth century, it was more important as a centre for line fishing, mainly for haddock and cod. In this picture fishermen on the quay are baiting 'snoods' on wooden frames. A hundred of these 'snoods' were attached to each 50-fathom (300-foot) line. The lines were then laid in flat baskets known as 'sculls' (two of which are visible here), so that they could be run out cleanly as the boat went ahead.

Opposite: **Fisherman at Bosham,** *c.* **1910**

Photographer unknown

Posed perhaps rather self-consciously, this study by an anonymous photographer nonetheless forms a charming tableau of a grizzled old fisherman entrancing a group of children with tales of the sea. It is one of a series of studies of the fisherfolk of Bosham, at that time home to a small but thriving fishing community on the south coast near Chichester.

A study of two fishermen

Fishermen tanning nets

Women in the curing shed, Burnmouth

Washing day at Ross

Scenes at Burnmouth and Ross, Berwickshire, 1884
Photographer unknown

These six views, part of a larger series of some fifty images, give a rare glimpse into the daily life of a small fishing community in the late nineteenth century. The village and harbour of Burnmouth and Ross lie close to each other at the base of 200-foot cliffs a few miles north of Berwick-upon-Tweed. Physically scarcely changed in the course of the past century, there is now little sign of the fishing activity that was the original mainstay of the villages' existence. In the 1850s twenty-one large and thirty small boats, manned by 115 hands, sailed from the busy enclosed harbour, while ashore there lived curers and coopers, gutters and packers, and over 200

net-makers. Haddock and cod were caught on long lines and sent by road to Edinburgh, while the herring season lasted from July to September. These photographs were taken at the height of the Scottish fishing industry's prosperity, although the village had suffered terribly only a few years before in the great storm of 1881. Berwickshire was particularly severely hit, and of the forty-five fifies that sailed from harbours along the coast on a calm October day, only twenty-six managed to run back to Eyemouth. A hundred and eighty-nine men were lost from the boats in a few hours, among them twenty-four men from Burnmouth and Ross.

Above: **An old shanty at Ross**

Below: **A girl at the well**

***Opposite above:* The herring fleet at Scarborough, September 1897**
Photographer unknown

This scene vividly illustrates the strength of the sailing fishing industry of a century ago, as the herring fleet prepares to set sail from Scarborough in the last years of the century. The turn of the new century was to see a rapid growth in steam-powered fishing, and within a decade or so sights like this had become part of history. As the bathing machines in the foreground remind us, Scarborough was also Britain's first seaside resort, and even by the time this photograph was taken its importance as a fishing port was declining in favour of Hull and Grimsby.

***Opposite below:* Mevagissey, *c.* 1900**
Photographer unknown

Scenes such as this, showing Mevagissey harbour crowded with fishing boats, were a common sight in fishing ports throughout the British Isles at this period. The boats seen here, with their single lugsail and the square stern characteristic of east Cornish vessels, were known as 'toshers' at Mevagissey, and most ran to a maximum length of 19 feet 11 inches in order to avoid increased harbour dues payable on boats above 20 feet.

***Above:* The Plymouth trawler *Lile* (PH 347) at Plymouth, October 1933**
Photographer unknown

This view of the ketch-rigged Plymouth trawler *Lile*, built in 1894, gives a clear idea of the sturdy yet graceful lines of these boats. A powerful sail plan and heavy construction were necessary to tow the trawling gear, and this boat also has auxiliary engine power. Until the last quarter of the nineteenth century most trawlers were single-masted cutter-rigged boats, but in later years the two-masted ketch rig, which divided the sail area and did away with the long boom of the cutter, became accepted as easier to handle.

TRADE AND EMPIRE

Loading tea at Colombo for export to England, 1880s
Photograph by William L. H. Skeen and Co.

In a ringing declaration extolling Birmingham's industrial pre-eminence, written at about the time of Queen Victoria's Golden Jubilee in 1887, an inhabitant of that city painted a glowing picture of its (and by extension Great Britain's) indispensable and expanding economic presence on the world stage:

> The Arab sheik eats his pilaf with a spoon from Birmingham. The Egyptian pasha takes his cup of sherbet on a Birmingham waiter . . . To feed and defend himself the Redskin uses a gun from Birmingham, the luxurious Hindu orders plate and lamps for table and drawing room . . . To the plains of South America, for the swift-riding horsemen, Birmingham despatches spurs, stirrup-leathers and burnished buttons; to the Colonies, for native planters, hatchets for cutting sugar cane, vats and presses . . .

These words (a portion of a much longer catalogue) proclaim, in terms no doubt a little complacent and pompous,

Opposite: **Loading timber at Sydney, *c.* 1905**

Photographer unknown

The steamer *Darius* is being loaded with railway sleepers for export to South Africa. The *Darius*, a 3,295 ton steamer built in 1892, was owned by Archibald Currie & Co. Currie had started as a coastal trader in the China Sea and New Zealand before founding his own shipping business in 1862, concentrating largely on the colonial trade with India. He later became one of the most powerful business magnates in Australia, and was a powerful advocate for the introduction of Asian labour in the development of Northern Australia.

a real pride in Great Britain's economic achievements in the course of the nineteenth century and mainly during the preceding fifty years of Victoria's reign. The productions of Birmingham and the other industrial cities of Manchester and Glasgow had placed Great Britain at the zenith of her industrial achievement, in a position of dominance over the world economy never before and never since achieved. And in order to sell cloth, iron, machinery and coal, and to import in turn food and other raw materials, Britain had built up the largest merchant fleet in the world. In 1870 the shipping of the British Empire – including both sail and steam – accounted for around half of the combined tonnage of the world's major maritime nations, and by 1890 this had risen to nearer 63 per cent. By the turn of the century the peak had been reached and these figures were slowly declining, but Britain remained the world's principal maritime nation until after the Second World War (although the United States possessed a greater tonnage of laid-up shipping).

Britain's economic power in the last quarter of the nineteenth century was closely linked with her colonial trade; the expansion of the British Empire in the years following the Napoleonic Wars created the conditions through which Britain came to control a worldwide web of commerce. Actual British territorial gains from the peace of 1815 were not large, but in fact colonial expansion was a process already well under way by the time the conflict ended. For even during the great struggle against Revolutionary and Napoleonic France,

Britain was also engaged in conflicts with the empires of other European nations – in the Caribbean, at the Cape of Good Hope and in the Far East. Defence and commerce were intimately connected in these hostilities, and concurrent domestic population growth added further expansionist pressures. Population increased threefold from 6.5 to 18 million between 1750 and 1850, and the years after 1815 saw a period of large-scale emigration from Britain in response to poverty and increasing industrialization.

But in 1815 Great Britain as yet stood only on the threshold of empire. Her largest possessions were in British North America, her territories on the Indian sub-continent which had already been the scene of bitter struggles with France, Cape Colony, her Caribbean colonies and the narrow settled portion along the eastern seaboard of Australia. Her remaining colonial territories were mainly small islands of strategic rather than economic importance, such as St Helena, Mauritius, Malta and Gibraltar.

By the time of Queen Victoria's Diamond Jubilee some eighty years later in 1897, Great Britain had made massive territorial advances: British India had become an empire and her boundaries had grown to include Burma, while the South-east Asian archipelago had been effectively divided between British and Dutch spheres of control. The whole of Australia, New Zealand and the eastern half of New Guinea were now parts of the empire, while Cape Colony had, in the process of becoming the South African Republic, absorbed huge tracts of territory to the north. The continent as a whole was in the throes of the European 'scramble for Africa', and by the century's end Britain's territorial advances had achieved commercial predominance over western and southern Africa, while Egypt, the strategic lynchpin to the north, was controlled by Britain in all but name.

This colonial expansion had a slow start, however, and British shipping declined by some 12 per cent in the long depression that followed the Napoleonic Wars. For a period a general movement towards free trade was reversed to protect British shipping and living standards, and heavy tariffs were imposed on imported grain. The 1815 Corn Laws affected commercial policy for the next thirty years, but by the 1840s the conventional economic wisdom of both parties in Parliament was that free trade offered the best prospect for Britain's prosperity as a manufacturing and trading nation. In 1843 Canadian wheat was allowed into Britain virtually free of customs duties and in 1846 Peel, using the famine in Ireland as a lever, passed legislation repealing the Corn Laws. The succeeding Liberal administration eliminated almost all the

existing preferences in favour of colonial products and repealed the Navigation Acts which had restricted the carrying of goods into British ports to British registered ships. While the colonies (particularly the sugar-growing lobby) resented for a time the end of preferential tariffs, the repeal of the Navigation Acts, which among other things reduced transport costs, was generally welcomed. Remaining preferences were removed between 1853 and 1860, by which time the colonies were treated for economic purposes in much the same way as foreign countries. Not all benefited equally, of course, and the altruism of empire was a strictly limited concept. One need only look at India where, in the name of free trade, the mill owners of northern England ruthlessly flooded the market with cheap textiles, thereby destroying a staple domestic industry. The growth of British shipping in the following decades, however, has often been accounted for by the abolition of these acts, and while they had a stimulating effect on colonial trade in the long run, they had in fact already been much eroded in the previous decades, with the signing of agreements allowing American ships carrying American produce to trade with British possessions. This and other concessions meant that half of British trade was already governed by exceptions to the Navigation Acts.

One of the great stimulators of late nineteenth-century trade was the construction of the Suez Canal, opened in 1869, which cut the voyage to the Far East by over 3,000 miles and saved ten or more days steaming time. Within a few years the route was covered by bunkering stations at intervals which further worked to the advantage of steam – although for some bulk cargoes, as has been noted earlier, the journey by sail round the Cape was still an economic proposition.

Ironically enough, Palmerston had at first tried to stop the Egyptian government from letting de Lesseps's company build the canal, because he felt that it would inevitably lead to greater British involvement in Egypt and that the increased shipping traffic would highlight French influence in the area. In addition, it was feared that the canal would weaken the economic position of South Africa at an already difficult period by diverting eastbound trade. But the canal was built, although it took the American Civil War and increased demand for Egyptian cotton to nurse the scheme through a funding crisis. British shipping in the 1860s was also able to take advantage of the American Civil War, which severely damaged the American shipping economy, and the opening of the Suez Canal at the end of the decade helped the already developing trade with Britain's eastern colonies. Once the canal was in fact open, the new British Prime Minister Benjamin Disraeli, a more wholehearted imperialist than his predecessor, accepted the self-evident British involvement in the affairs of Egypt, particularly since three-quarters of the shipping using the canal was British. By the early 1870s the Khedive's lavish lifestyle had exhausted his assets, and in 1875 Disraeli was able to purchase from him nearly half the shares of the Suez Canal Company for £4 million. While this did not give the British government voting control over the affairs of the company, it allowed Britain to assert its interest in Egypt and to protect its eastern trade.

And in the east the effect of the opening of the canal was certainly a momentous event. In Singapore, for instance, trade throughout the 1860s had been sluggish, but in January 1870 the editor of the *Straits Times* was able to comment on two events which 'will fill important pages in the world's history and will mark the year 1869 as the beginning of a new era in the lives of the great maritime and commercial nations'. These two events were the opening of the canal and the Pacific Railway across America. In large measure this optimism was justified and the canal revived the settlement's flagging trade. In particular it allowed the Tanjong Pagar Dock Company to expand and build new facilities at New Harbour, precipitating a number of reclamation schemes that allowed Singapore to benefit fully from the revival in trade.

Technological development and expansion of steamer fleets were also encouraged from the 1840s by mail contracts placed by the government, which were effectively a form of subsidy to strategically placed companies, such as Cunard on its North Atlantic route and P&O's to the Far East. While stimulating growth, this move also gave the Admiralty access to a pool of steamers for use in emergencies. By 1853, steam packet companies with mail subsidies owned about half the registered steam tonnage on the register. As a result of these subsidies the African Steam Ship Company was able to provide a monthly service to the West African colonies from 1851, while P&O established the first mail service to Australia in the following year. Similarly, in 1856 the Allan Line turned over to steam for the Quebec service, and in 1857 the Union Steamship Company won the mail contract to South Africa. By 1860 the government was spending over £1 million a year on these mail contracts.

A further major stimulus to the expansion of international maritime trade was the laying of submarine cables. In the present age of sophisticated communications it is perhaps difficult to appreciate the significance of the submarine cable system, although some idea of its contemporary impact may be gauged from the fact that Rudyard Kipling was moved to write a poem on the subject ('Here in the womb of the world . . . Men talk to-day o'er the waste of the ultimate slime'). The first successful cable crossed the English Channel in 1851, but technical problems hindered expansion until the following decade, when the government of India's Persian Gulf Line was laid in 1863 and two Atlantic cables were opened in 1866. There followed a surge of telegraph laying which lasted until the middle of the following decade, with India linked to Malaya in 1875 and Australia and New Zealand joined in 1876. This activity was partly stimulated by government subsidies to companies opening cables in areas 'most called for by imperial and commercial interests', and by the end of the century Britain owned about 60 per cent of the world's submarine cables, in particular through the giant Eastern Telegraph Company, which dominated everywhere but the North Atlantic.

The submarine telegraph profoundly affected commerce. By making market information rapidly available it increased competition and brought down prices. And access to accurate information encouraged specialization, allowing merchants to hold smaller stocks and thus tie up less capital. As ever, trade and imperial defence were interdependent, and the cables had major implications for planning since they facilitated military and fleet movements and co-ordination.

The ways by which the empire grew in the course of the century were many and various – whether by right of conquest, settlement or discovery – but on the part of government at least, deliberate imperial expansion was only rarely a preferred option. British interests, both commercial and territorial, must be protected and this inevitably led from time to time to the acquisition of new territories, whether in response to indigenous hostility to British commerce, or to forestall the imperial pretensions of European rivals. But wherever possible the government preferred the expense of colonial expansion to fall on the shoulders of private enterprise. One method of effecting this was the granting of royal charters to private companies and investors to exploit new territories and set up administrations.

The chartering of private companies has of course had a long and venerable history. The possession of India had come about through the trading activities of the East India Company, while vast tracts of the Canadian wilderness had been opened up by the Hudson's Bay Company. The late nineteenth century saw a resurgence of such activity, if on a smaller scale. In West Africa, for instance, merchants had traded with the kingdoms of native rulers in the great Niger delta for years without need of formal protection from their governments. But the colonial activities of the French, German and Belgian governments in West and central Africa prompted a British response. Almost all the British companies trading in palm oil were under the control of (Sir) George Goldie and in 1886, after several rebuffs, he was granted a royal charter with powers of government in the Niger basin north of the coastal region. By using his powers to create a monopoly of trade on the river, Goldie was able to generate sufficient income both to pay the costs of his administration and to make a profit: similar trading-cum-administrative operations were practised as far afield as British North Borneo and East Africa. By such means the home government was able to take full trading advantage of overseas territories without shouldering the electorally unpopular financial responsibilities of maintaining colonies. For the British public was notoriously fickle, and jingoistic enthusiasm for the Greater Britain beyond the seas could rapidly turn to hostility against administrations who it was felt were sacrificing the interests (and spending the taxes) of the British elector in favour of overseas territories.

Sometimes a mixture of private concerns and government officials co-operated in exploiting the natural resources of potentially lucrative territories. Commercial relations with the Burmese empire had existed – with varying degrees of amicability – since the early days of the East India Company, when in 1617 agents were sent to Syriam and Pegu. Burmese teak was renowned and many fine sailing ships in the mid nineteenth century were built at Moulmein, where Duncan Dunbar had opened a shipyard in the 1830s, while the ruby mines and rich rice yields of Upper Burma attracted the attentions of European merchants. By gradual encroachment and three wars the whole of Burma had been absorbed into British India by 1886. The third war had been precipitated largely by commercial interests intent on opening up the length of the Irrawaddy River to European trade as well as by suspicions about French ambitions in the area. Between 1859 and 1865 navigation on the Irrawaddy was undertaken by steamers of the Bengal Marine, but in that latter year the Irrawaddy Flotilla and Burmese Steam Navigation Company (from 1875 the Irrawaddy Flotilla Company) was formed to implement a contract with the government of India for the conveyance of troops, mail and general traffic between Rangoon and Mandalay. Although the company was run on a commercial basis many of its functions were quasi-administrative. Apart from the transport of mails, the company maintained a small fleet of vessels for river work and

channel marking and in later years even instituted an air service. The company was an integral component of the Burmese economy and at its height operated the largest river fleet in the world: by 1938 this comprised over 600 vessels, from large paddle steamers to buoying launches and lighters; and most of these were manufactured by the shipbuilding firm of William Denny of Dumbarton and shipped out in pieces to the company shipyards in Burma. Although the company continued to exist until 1950, most of its fleet was scuttled in the face of the Japanese invasion of Burma in 1942.

Government might also be forced to take on new responsibilities against its will when trading colonies were formed in defiance of the home government. In the days of slow communications a man of confidence and vision had considerable scope for unrestricted action. Such a figure was Sir Stamford Thomas Raffles, afire with a vision of Britain's imperial destiny. Determined to forestall Dutch ambitions and to secure British control in South-east Asia, in 1819 he negotiated the purchase of the island of Singapore from the local ruler. Although this unilateral act was a source of intense displeasure to his masters in the East India Company (and of fury to the Dutch), the island remained in British hands and in a few decades Singapore, operating on free trade principles as an open port, had become the most important entrepôt port of the east. Situated in the most favourable position on the route to the east, the island rapidly eclipsed Penang and Malacca, the two other British outposts that formed the Straits Settlements, and established a commercial supremacy that has continued to the present day. The other great commercial centre of the east, Hong Kong, had also been founded as a result of British overseas trade. Acquired at the end of the Opium War of 1839–42, it became an important entrepôt for Britain's expanding trade with China from the 1860s onwards. And although Britain's dominance in China was declining at the turn of the century, British shipping carried most of China's foreign trade.

One of Great Britain's most successful trading partnerships that developed in the course of the nineteenth century was the relationship with Australia. The beginnings were not auspicious, and Australia's main attraction was originally perceived to be that of distance and suitability as a dumping ground for criminals. The first batch of convicts arrived at Sydney Cove in 1788, and it was soon realized that the settlement would not survive without some measure of support from the home country. Sydney soon became the centre for the South Pacific whaling trade, but this was not enough to support the colony and it continued to need financial assistance from England for many years. But with the gradual freeing of the convicts into the nascent community, the development of Sydney and the expansion beyond the natural boundary of the Blue Mountains, the colony gradually started to look as if it might become self-sufficient. Convict transportation to New South Wales ended in principle in 1840 (although the last convict ship was not to sail until 1868), by which time about 150,000 prisoners had been transported. But Australia had been receiving voluntary as well as convict immigrants from the 1820s, and the opening up of the country to agricultural exploitation was boosted by railway construction from mid century onwards. But it was the discovery of gold in 1851, first in New South Wales and then in much larger quantities in Victoria a few months later, that provided the tremendous attraction that lured thousands to Australia. In the course of the 1850s the population rose from 400,000 to 1.1 million and in the following decades Australia was swept forward in a burst of prosperity, based first on gold and then on other minerals such as copper, lead and silver. Prosperity came to Victoria, and particularly to the business and shipping centre of Melbourne. These conditions attracted further emigration and investment from the home country, and in the 1880s Australia drew ahead of Canada in the number of its inhabitants who were of British descent. But the end of the decade saw the end of the boom years. New South Wales, which alone of the Australian colonies had maintained a free trade economy, again came to the fore as a large-scale exporter competing in world markets. Exports of wool, wheat and coal maintained a healthy maritime traffic, and while the opening of the Suez Canal had inevitably led to an increase in steamers, the long haul from Australia to Europe via the Cape with high-bulk cargoes gave a new lease of life to a generation of sailing ships.

The introduction of refrigeration also had important economic benefits to trade with the colonies. While the principle of refrigeration was well known, the machinery used produced a good deal of heat and was considered dangerous to use on board wooden ships. But once the iron ships became common, businessmen in the colonies started to export frozen foodstuffs to England. Successful early voyages in the 1880s paved the way for a great influx of produce that continues to the present day. Lamb and butter from New Zealand and Australia, fruit from the Cape and bacon from Canada made a significant contribution to the improvement of British working-class living standards. These refrigerated goods were not the only foods which improved transport was bringing to Britain in ever-increasing quantities. The

monopoly of tea production held by China in the early nineteenth century was displaced and by 1890 most of the tea on the world market was imported either from India, where it had been introduced in the 1830s, or from Ceylon (Sri Lanka), where it had first been extensively planted in the 1860s and 70s after the coffee industry had been destroyed by disease. The growth of the tea industry in Ceylon, together with its spice exports, stimulated export trade and led to major harbour improvements at Colombo in the 1880s.

By the end of the century British and empire shipping circled the globe in a dense pattern of trade between the colonies and the mother country: palm oil from West Africa, rice and timber from Burma, tin and later rubber from Malaya, wheat, meat and dairy produce from Canada, Australia and New Zealand, all crossed the oceans to spin the intricate web of seaborne trade. Among the innumerable publications celebrating Queen Victoria's Diamond Jubilee in 1897 was a lavish collection of photographic illustrations entitled *The Queen's Empire*. Organized in chapters illustrating such themes as trade, travel and the armed forces, the propagandist thrust of the work is revealed in H.O. Arnold-Foster's introduction, which paints a hopelessly idealistic picture of unity in diversity, with all the different races and cultures of the empire united in a common purpose. Behind all the variety,

> in every part of the Empire we shall find some trace of the work which Britain is doing throughout the world – the work of civilizing, of governing, of protecting life and property, and of extending the benefits of trade and commerce . . .

The confidence of such sentiments commands a measure of respect, even if we view such photographs in a more dispassionate light today. The dissolution of the British Empire, and a more objective evaluation of its motives, must inevitably modify our acceptance of such declarations. But whatever our historical perspective, few would deny that such images offer vivid and compelling evidence of a remarkably energetic and exciting period of history that helped to shape the modern world.

San Francisco, looking towards the Golden Gate, 1870
Photograph by Eadweard Muybridge
This photograph gives a deceptively peaceful and suburban air to the city of San Francisco in a view that looks out towards the Golden Gate and the Pacific beyond. The city at this period was in fact renowned for the rowdiness of its waterfront area and for the activities of the crimps who supplied crews to outgoing vessels.

Opposite below: **Whalers being refitted at Jarrow's Shipyard, Esquimalt, British Columbia, c. 1910**
Photographer unknown
The whaling grounds of the north-western Pacific had first been brought to European notice by Captain Cook's description of the area's natural resources, and from the 1790s until the middle of the present century these seas were a major source of whales. Further stimulus was provided to the industry by the introduction, spear-headed by British Columbia, of steam-driven whalers and processing plants in the early 1900s.

Above: **The Red River Transportation Company steamer**
***Dakota* at Dufferin, Manitoba, *c.* 1872**
Photograph by the Royal Engineers
Settlements had been established in the Red River area on land acquired from the Hudson's Bay Company by the Earl of Selkirk from 1811 onwards, and in the early years the area was settled largely by victims of the Highland clearances. Shallow draught paddle steamers run by private companies formed the principal means of communication and movement of produce for many isolated settlements in colonial territories.

Above: **The cod flakes at St John's, Newfoundland,** *c.* **1900**
Photograph by Simeon H. Parsons

This view looks along the straits from the narrow harbour entrance towards the town of St John's, with Newfoundlanders laying cod out to dry on the wooden flakes in a manner little changed for hundreds of years. The rich fishing grounds of the Newfoundland Banks have been a magnet to the fishing fleets of Europe from the sixteenth to the present century, and by 1610, the year in which a permanent English settlement was first planted on Newfoundland, some 200 ships were crossing from England each year. As well as earning foreign currency from the sale of fish to the Catholic countries of southern Europe, the Newfoundland fisheries were early recognized as a 'nursery' for the Royal Navy, for which they provided experienced crews in time of war.

Opposite above: **Splitting and gutting cod before drying, St John's, Newfoundland,** *c.* **1900**
Photograph by Simeon H. Parsons

Opposite below: **Weighing dried cod before packing, St John's, Newfoundland,** *c.* **1900**
Photograph by Simeon H. Parsons

**Opposite above: Men from HMS *Revenge* at Colón,
Panama, January 1870**
Photographer unknown
Before the construction of the Panama Canal, a railway across the
isthmus linked the Atlantic and Pacific Oceans. Here the officers
and crew of HMS *Revenge* are seen boarding a train at Colón on
the Caribbean coast to take them to their new ship, HMS *Zealous*,
moored at Panama on the Pacific.

Opposite below: Miraflores Lock, Panama Canal, May 1911
Photographer unknown
After his triumph at Suez, de Lesseps bankrupted himself in an
attempt to build a Panama Canal in the 1880s. It was not until 1904
that work started under American supervision to build a waterway

across the isthmus, and the massive project was completed in 1914
at a total cost of $352 million. This view shows work in progress
on the double Miraflores Lock, the last lock on the Pacific side of
the canal. In the background is one of the vast cranes mounted on
gantries which laid concrete in place.

**Above: HMS *New Zealand* passing through the
San Miguel Lock, Panama Canal, December 1919**
Photographer unknown
The 18,000 ton battlecruiser HMS *New Zealand* was the first British
naval vessel of any size to pass through the canal. This was during
Earl Jellicoe's British Empire tour of 1919–20, to confer on naval
co-operation. Jellicoe was not on board at this point, as he travelled
overland from Esquimalt and rejoined the ship at Key West.

Aberdeen Docks, Hong Kong, after the typhoon, September 1874

Photographer unknown

This panoramic view shows the docks after the great typhoon of 23–4 September in which thirty-five European ships were destroyed and 2,000 lives lost in six hours. Hong Kong's first dry dock was built at Aberdeen in about 1857 by the Scottish merchant and ship-builder Douglas Lapraik, who had lived in the East since the early 1840s. In 1865 it was absorbed into the Hong Kong and Whampoa Dock Company, a business established in 1863 by some of the most influential figures in Hong Kong commercial circles and which grew into the most powerful shipbuilding and repairing company in the colony.

Right: **Tanjong Pagar Docks, Singapore, 1890s**

Photograph by G. R. Lambert and Co.

The Tanjong Pagar Dock Company, which was later to evolve into today's Port of Singapore Authority, was formed in 1864 in response to the inadequate dock facilities then available on the island. An American-built barque is shown berthed in the Victoria Dock, the company's first dry dock, opened in 1868. The Tanjong Pagar Dock Company swallowed all its rivals in succeeding years until 1913, when it was transformed into the Singapore Harbour Board, a corporate statutory body maintaining its own police, fire and other services.

Opposite above: Ferry in Sydney harbour, 1870s
Photographer unknown
Until the completion of the Sydney Harbour Bridge in 1932, the only practical way to travel between north and south Sydney was by ferry. A limited service had been in operation as early as 1789 and the first paddle steamer, the *Surprise*, ran between Sydney and Parramatta in 1831. By the time this photograph was taken the busy harbour traffic was supporting more than sixty ferries running to various locations.

Below: View on the River Murray at Echuca, Victoria, with steamers unloading, c. 1875
Photograph by Nicholas Caire
By the mid 1870s over 400 steamers and 1,000 barges were operating on the River Murray to transport the colony of Victoria's growing traffic in wool, timber and other produce. This view shows the railway wharf built by the government at Echuca for the onward transport of the wool clip by land.

Opposite below: Sandridge Pier, Melbourne, c. 1870
Photograph by Samuel Clifford
Unlike Sydney, Brisbane and Hobart, Melbourne did not possess the advantage of good natural harbour facilities and for many years vessels of deep draught had to anchor and unload off-shore. The inadequacy of the shallow and narrow River Yarra as the port for a growing city became acute after the discovery of gold in 1851.

Little effective work had been done to remedy the situation when this photograph, showing the Melbourne and Hobson's Bay United Railway Company pier, was taken. It was not until Sir John Coode presented his scheme for harbour improvements in 1879 that work was put in hand to lay the foundations of the present-day port.

119

***Below:* Labour ship at Fiji, *c.* 1885**
Photographer unknown
'Kanaka' labour had first been imported from the South Sea Islands to work on the plantations of Queensland in the 1860s, and this later developed into the notorious trade of the 'blackbirders', who recruited and often kidnapped islanders to work as indentured labour on Australian cotton and sugar plantations. International agitation brought the trade under official scrutiny, but only after areas of Melanesia had become seriously depopulated. In 1901 the Commonwealth Government legislated against blackbirding and laid down that such recruitment must cease by 1904, and by 1908 the last of the Kanakas had been returned to the islands.

***Opposite above:* The Irrawaddy Flotilla Company launch *Tai-Say-Galay* at Rangoon, Burma, *c.* 1880**
Photographer unknown
Rising in Tibet, the Irrawaddy runs the length of Burma to form one of the world's great river highways, and with the growth of British influence in that country the Irrawaddy Flotilla Company was established in 1865 to carry troops, mail and produce between Upper and Lower Burma. The fleet grew in time with Burma's commercial development and by 1938 comprised over 600 vessels, carrying over 8 million passengers and 1.5 million tons of cargo in a normal year.

***Opposite below:* The Irrawaddy Flotilla Company office at Bassein, Burma, *c.* 1890**
Photographer unknown
Situated on a tributary of the Irrawaddy to the west of Rangoon, Bassein was the location of a company branch office and was connected to the capital by a daily ferry service of double-decked creek steamers. Bassein boasted historical connections with the East India Company dating back to the seventeenth century, when a trading factory was located in the area.

Opposite above: **The clipper *Lady Egidea***
loading at Calcutta, March 1875
Photograph by Stretton
The elegant lines of the clipper are well displayed in this view of
the 1,239 ton ship *Lady Egidea*, moored at Calcutta. Built at Ardrossan in 1860, she continued in service until the early 1880s.

Opposite below: **The wreck of the *Thunder* after**
the Calcutta cyclone, 5 October 1864
Photograph by W. Fisk Williams or Wagentreiber
The busy port of Calcutta, situated nearly 100 miles from the sea
up the River Hooghly, was particularly susceptible to storms
between April and November. This view shows the wreck of the
steam opium clipper *Thunder*, which was driven onshore during the
ferocious cyclone which struck Calcutta on 5 October 1864. Several
hundred lives were lost, the southern and eastern suburbs of the
city were largely destroyed, and over 200 vessels were driven from
their moorings into a tangled mass of wreckage.

Above: **Building the Colombo Breakwater, Ceylon,**
March 1884
Photograph by William L. H. Skeen and Co.
The 'Titan' crane is here seen depositing 10-ton concrete bags along
the top of the sea berm. Work on this massive breakwater had
begun in 1874, after it had been decided that Colombo was the
island's most favourable location to attract the increased steamer
trade to the Far East promised by the opening of the Suez Canal.
Designed by the great harbour engineer Sir John Coode and built
largely with convict labour, the breakwater was completed in 1885
at a cost of £750,000.

Above: **Port Said and the Suez Canal, showing
the Suez Canal Company buildings, 1870s**

Photographer unknown

The idea of connecting Europe and Asia by a navigable waterway
dates back to the Pharaohs, but it was not until the mid nineteenth
century, with the increase of worldwide seaborne traffic and the
availability of appropriate technology, that the dream was realized.
The 100-mile canal was built between 1859 and 1869 by a company
managed by the engineer Ferdinand de Lesseps. The British, who
had resolutely attempted to obstruct its construction, soon realized
both the commercial and strategic importance of the canal, and in
1875 the Prime Minister, Benjamin Disraeli, secretly obtained a
controlling interest in the company on behalf of the government.

Opposite above: **Alexandria, 1870s**

Photograph by Bonfils

The two obelisks later known as Cleopatra's Needles were erected
at Heliopolis by the Pharaoh Thothmes III in about 1500 BC, and
had stood on the foreshore at Alexandria since being moved there
in about 15 BC. The transportation of one of the obelisks to London
encouraged the Americans to obtain its partner: this view shows
the standing needle that was taken to America and placed in Central
Park in New York in 1881.

Opposite below: **Transporting Cleopatra's Needle
from Alexandria to London, 29 August 1877**

Photograph by Borgiotti

The needle, presented to England as far back as 1820, lay half-
buried in the sands at Alexandria until 1877, when it was finally
brought to London after an incident-filled voyage. First, as seen
here, the iron hull encasing the needle was punctured by a rock as
it was rolled into the sea. Then the journey to Europe was dogged
by bad weather and during a storm in the Bay of Biscay in which
six men lost their lives, *Cleopatra* parted company with her towing
vessel *Olga*. The needle was not finally recaptured, towed to
London and erected on the Embankment until mid 1878.

**The sternwheeler *Hornbill* on the Eyong River at Okopedi,
Southern Nigeria, 1909**

Photographer unknown

The *Hornbill*, which came into service in 1906, was one of a fleet
of nineteen sternwheelers, steam pinnaces and motor boats which
transported produce and passengers to and from the West African
hinterland and the coast. The *Hornbill* was part of the Cross River
Transport Service, operated by Elder, Dempster & Co., and in 1909
she transported 6,233 passengers and 2,974 tons of cargo at a net
profit of £112.

Trader's warehouse at Opobo, Southern Nigeria, *c.* 1912
Photographer unknown
Situated at the mouth of the Imo River, Opobo became a centre of commercial importance in the palm oil trade. The area had risen to prominence under King Jaja, who in the 1870s created a monopoly much resented by the British. He was tried for blocking trade in 1887, and after his deportation to the West Indies his markets were taken over by European traders.

PAX BRITANNICA

THE NINETEENTH-CENTURY NAVY AND ITS LEGACY

Battleships of the Home Fleet in line ahead, 18 July 1935
Photograph by Francis Mortimer

The naval historian Sir William Laird Clowes, reporting Queen Victoria's Diamond Jubilee Naval Review in the *Illustrated London News*, wrote a report that expresses well the amalgam of motives that characterized the greatest display of naval strength the world had yet seen, in which 165 ships, including twenty-two battleships, forty cruisers and twenty torpedo boats, were gathered at Spithead at the end of June 1897:

. . . No review in Great Britain or abroad has ever been . . . so magnificent . . . It has been a day never to be forgotten. All who were present have come away with new ideas as to what this great Empire means both to us and to others; and it can hardly . . . fail in furthering to a very great degree the two principal objects for which it was arranged. One of these was to prove that Britain still rules the waves, and, moreover, intends to go on ruling them; the other was to show to our fellow subjects in the outlying parts of the Empire that they were with us in a common possession to be proud of and to depend upon in the hour of need.

The review was partly grateful celebration for sixty years of a reign slowly drawing towards its close, partly an aggressive display of bravado, and partly a gesture of solidarity with the Greater Britain beyond the seas. A final unstated component was an element of bluff, that essential constituent of the imperial ethos, for a number of the older ships on such proud display were incapable of steaming but had to be towed into position. But for the thousands who attended the spectacle and who watched the glittering display of the ships lit up at night, their form outlined in strings of lights, the Spithead review was an impressive and intimidating spectacle, particularly so as all the ships present were drawn from home waters, without recalling any vessels from foreign stations. Certainly the German observers present found it a disturbing demonstration of national power and swiftly responded to its implicit challenge. In 1898 the first German Navy Law was passed, setting in train the arms race that dominated the first decade of the new century and which was in succeeding years to see the erosion of the British maritime

Opposite: **Naval pensioners in the grounds of the Royal Naval Hospital, Greenwich, 1840s**
Photograph possibly by the Reverend Richard Calvert Jones

hegemony that had subsisted since 1815, the last year of the Napoleonic Wars.

The ending of hostilities with France in 1815 left Britain's navy in an unassailably dominant position, but much of the service, both the structure of the institution itself and many of the ships, was obsolete and inefficient. Ship design had changed little in the previous half-century, and conditions for the average seaman were often appalling, while the career structure for officers offered little encouragement to the talented and ambitious. Patronage and promotion by seniority led to a top-heavy structure that inhibited initiative and rewarded inertia: but the dead weight of tradition could not long withstand the march of technological progress which in the course of the century was to transform both the ships and weapons of the world's navies, and in its wake create a wholly new professional fighting force.

As with the merchant service, the great transformation of the nineteenth-century navy was the change from sail to steam power. Great birth-pains attended these changes, as slowly but surely the superiority of steam was demonstrated to often hostile forces within the Admiralty and Whitehall, men who saw centuries of tradition swept away in the dirt and noise of a technology that seemed to reduce the Senior Service to the status of a mechanized drayhorse. Such a radical metamorphosis – from the great bluff-sided 'wooden walls' of the first half of the century, designed to fire broadsides in the line of battle, to the steel battleships of the early twentieth century, built for speed, manoeuvrability and long-range battle – also had to overcome major technical problems. The second half of the century, therefore, was to see the introduction of a succession of novel vessel types which were swiftly superseded as designers and builders struggled to keep up with each new development in weaponry, engines, and building technology. Many of these changes were of kind rather than degree, processes not susceptible of evaluation and testing except by actual construction. Thus a bewildering variety of ships built to accommodate the latest thinking were constructed, tested, evolved and discarded. Some showed the way to the future, some were frankly unlovely and inelegant if utilitarian, some were blind alleys and a few were disasters. A few of these wrong turnings were technical hiccups, like the Armstrong breech-loading guns of the early 1860s, which performed unsatisfactorily and led the navy to abandon a clearly superior form of loading for over a decade. Others had tragic results, the most dramatic of which was perhaps the fate of HMS *Captain*, designed by Captain Cowper Coles with heavy turrets mounted on the

centreline of the ship and a low freeboard. Coles had the backing of a number of influential figures, including the Prince Consort, and HMS *Captain* was built despite the strong misgivings of the Admiralty. In September 1870, only six months after the completion of her trials, *Captain* heeled over in a squall in the Bay of Biscay with the loss of all but eighteen of her complement of 500 officers and men. The subsequent committee of inquiry into the disaster established that *Captain* had capsized due to the lack of stability inherent in a full-rigged ship with a low freeboard and heavy, centrally mounted armaments. Coles (who went down with his ship) was a pioneer in his championing of the turret gun, which was indeed the way of the future, but this unhappy combination of old and new technology graphically illustrated the uneven pace of change and an uncertain mastery of the new skills required.

The age of steam had come to the Royal Navy in 1822 when its first successful steamship, the *Comet*, was launched. But this and other early vessels, with their heavy, unreliable engines, were generally lightly armed and restricted to use as tugs and auxiliaries. All these powered vessels were paddle steamers, which in addition to their inherent locomotive inefficiency suffered both from the vulnerability of the exposed paddle sponsons to enemy fire and from the limited space available for armaments, rendering paddle propulsion unsuitable for larger fighting vessels. From 1836 onwards Francis Pettit Smith attempted to prove to the Admiralty the superiority of his newly patented screw propeller, but despite several demonstrations, the innate conservatism of the Admiralty refused to be fully convinced of its superiority. Only after the dramatic tug of war of 1845, when the propeller-driven *Rattler* dragged the paddle steamer *Alecto* along at a steady 2½ knots, was the supremacy of the propeller conceded. It was not until the 1880s, however, that increased reliability and efficiency of the triple-expansion engine paved the way for the complete abandonment of sails.

The Crimean War, the only major international conflict in which the navy was involved between the Napoleonic Wars and the First World War, was to have a critical effect on the development of naval vessels. For the British and French the Crimean War was one of blockade, but on 30 November 1853, in the only major fleet action of the war, a Turkish squadron was burnt to the waterline off Sinope in a few minutes by a much smaller Russian force armed with shell-firing guns. The only ships available for Britain's war effort in the Crimea were old ships of the line, and as they were towed into position by tugs these bulky and ponderous 'wooden walls' were easy targets for shore batteries; while no major vessels were lost there were several near misses. These demonstrations of the vulnerability of wooden ships against shellfire were to be crucial factors in hastening the introduction of iron as a building material.

The French response to the requirement in the Crimea for a shallow draft armoured craft that could close with shore emplacements was the 'floating battery', and these vessels were the precursor of the ironclad. Of composite construction, with iron plates laid on a wooden hull, they successfully demonstrated the armoured ship's ability to take the battle close to the enemy with a fair degree of invulnerability. Meanwhile, the British answer was the gunboat, of which more than 160 had been built by the end of the war. These 100-foot wooden boats, three-masted and armed with one 68-pounder and one 32-pounder gun, were later to prove their worth in countless colonial skirmishes and small wars. For the rest of the century 'gunboat diplomacy' was to be a prominent weapon in the navy's role as policeman of the seas and guardian of commerce. From the pirate-infested waters of South-east Asia to the great trading rivers of West Africa, a swift and mobile force could be brought to bear whenever the rights of legitimate commerce were questioned.

The lessons learned in the Crimea were not lost on the French and they quickly set about the production of an armour-clad warship. The *Gloire*, a wooden-hulled ship with an outer skin of iron, was launched in 1859 but her supremacy was short-lived, for 1861 saw the completion of the iron-hulled *Warrior*. Faster, more heavily armed and better armoured than her French rival, she re-established British naval supremacy at a stroke. She was also as revolutionary in her way as the *Dreadnought* was to be forty years later, both in the material of her construction and in her form, which looked forward to the modern battleship. The *Warrior* also saw the real start of the superiority of technology in the race for naval supremacy and Britain was doubly lucky in having a merchant service already at the forefront of iron and steel shipbuilding. Many of these vessels – like HMS *Warrior* herself – were built in private yards and by 1865 Britain had thirty ironclads in commission against France's eighteen.

The spiralling onward rush of technology created its own impetus, but its effects were exacerbated in the field of national defence, where each new advance provoked its own response. The speed of these changes was largely beyond the control of individual nations, and in their turn they created a new kind of naval officer, a generation of technocrats who were excited by the new possibilities and challenges offered by science. This was particularly true in the field of gunnery, where each new development in power and accuracy led to a response in the form of faster, more heavily armed and armoured ships. From the invention of the explosive shell in 1830 to the rifled, breech-loading, rapid-fire guns of the early twentieth century, the increasing efficiency and firepower of weaponry placed their own unarguable demands on the design of the navy's ships. HMS *Warrior*, for example, the pride of Britain's navy in 1861, became effectively obsolete the following year when an Armstrong gun was demonstrated whose 300-pound shell could pierce her hull. And so the contest continued: as each more powerful gun was developed, warship designers produced more heavily armoured ships, although to maintain mobility they were often forced to reduce the armoured area.

The very speed of technological change, and the massive capital investment it demanded, meant that as the century wore on no one nation could expect to retain an indefinite paramountcy, although it was several decades before Great Britain was fully to accept this inevitability. As early as the 1880s the growth of other industrial powers was beginning to encroach on Britain's assumed right to rule the waves. In 1884, a series of articles in the *Pall Mall Gazette*, based on material supplied by Captain 'Jacky' Fisher and entitled *The Truth about the Navy*, shattered some of the complacency of those who proudly surveyed the empire and assumed that Britain's colonial dependencies nestled snug and secure beneath the shielding wing of the mother country. Further ammunition for parties lobbying for increased naval expenditure was supplied by the deliberations of the Carnarvon Commission, formed in 1879 to investigate Britain's imperial defences. Its conclusions were shattering: defences of the British overseas bases were nugatory, while the navy itself, if put to the test, would be incapable of defending the sealanes against a determined threat.

The plans drawn up to remedy this situation formed the basis of the most important piece of naval legislation of the late nineteenth century, the Naval Defence Act of 1889. The 'Two Power Standard' of equivalent strength to the navies of the next two most powerful nations (France and Russia) became an explicit foundation of policy and led to a massive construction programme costing £21.5 million over a five-year period. At the top end of the programme came the *Royal Sovereign* class of battleship, soon to be followed by even larger classes. Distinguished by their heavy armour, high speed and wide range, they were designed to engage the enemy outside torpedo or ramming range in all seas. Over forty cruisers with light armour protection took over the task of world-wide commerce protection, while from 1893 lightly armoured high-speed torpedo-boat-destroyers took on the task of battlefleet protection. By the turn of the century the overseas bases had also been overhauled and – linked by telegraph – Singapore, the Cape, Alexandria, Gibraltar and Dover formed a world-wide network protecting British interests. These, in Fisher's exultant boast, were the 'Five strategic keys [that] lock up the world'.

But the new century and the quickening of the arms race with Germany were to alter this balance fundamentally. Britain, as the cradle of the industrial revolution, had been the first to take advantage of the technological benefits it offered; but this lead had been slowly eroded and other nations, some with greater resources of raw material at their disposal, were set to take up the challenge. First among these was Germany, which had taken fright at Britain's display of might at Spithead in 1897 and was determined to redress the balance. But at the beginning of the new century these clouds were small on the horizon, and even a man as prescient as Fisher, expounding his views on imperial defence in 1900, was able to argue for a policy of 'Imperial isolation' for the navy, believing that Britain's maritime strength could be maintained without formal alliances, but through sheer superiority in force of arms and striking power. But the rise of the new naval powers was ultimately to expose the impossibility of such a stance. The industrial strength of the United States and Germany, bolstered by the development of railway systems, the rapid growth of the Japanese navy and Russia's new base at Port Arthur, all introduced new unknowns into the equation of the maritime balance of power. By now the German threat was becoming fully evident and its implications frighteningly clear. The methodical expansion of the German navy, which had been set in train by naval acts in the last years of the nineteenth century, was inevitably directed against Great Britain rather than her continental neighbours, and this led Britain into a series of alliances with France, Japan and the United States. Within five years of Fisher's boast of 'Imperial isolation', the rising tide of Germany's expansion had forced Great Britain to concede that in a modern world of rapid technological advance no one nation could stand alone and pre-eminent on the oceans of the world. If Britannia still wished to rule the waves, she must now do so in partnership with other nations against Germany.

But if Fisher had misjudged the speed of change in 1900, it was he more than any other single individual who created

the twentieth-century navy and whose legacy survived up to the Second World War and beyond. Indefatigable, charming, quite ruthless and an administrator of genius, he forced through change at every level. Fascinated by technology and its implications for naval power and determined to create the most efficient fighting force in the world, he was quite unencumbered by sentimental attachments to the old navy. His period as First Sea Lord from 1904 to 1910 was characterized by wholesale reform, not only in the modernization of the fleet itself but also in the training and organization of its officers and men. But of all his reforms, perhaps none was more far-reaching than his creation of the 'all big-gun' battleship, the *Dreadnought*.

As with the ships, so with the men. Technology had placed huge demands on naval personnel, forcing them in the space of fifty years to abandon generations of hard-earned expertise and to learn entirely new skills and organizational techniques. As the full-rigged sailing ship passed into history, new skills came into being. The year of Queen Victoria's accession, 1837, had seen the creation of an engineering branch of the navy (where previously the manufacturers had supplied technicians for the lowly task of maintaining the noisy, hissing monsters), and in 1840 a naval gunnery school, HMS *Excellent*, was installed on board the former ship of the line *Queen Charlotte* in Portsmouth harbour. This was the first Naval Technical School and signalled a turning away from the traditional training methods of the old navy towards greater specialization to meet the new demands of the age. In 1877, largely due to Fisher's forward thinking, a torpedo branch also became part of *Excellent*'s programme. The increasing professionalism of the navy was also seen in the adoption of a standard uniform in 1855, while higher education for officers was supplied at the Royal Naval College at Greenwich from 1873. The ubiquitous Fisher was responsible also for the founding of HMS *Dartmouth* and HMS *Osborne* as training establishments with more democratic entrance policies and by the turn of the century the Royal Navy had become a truly professional organization.

The forty years since the launch of the *Warrior* in 1860 had been a period of intense experimentation in every area of naval warfare. It had seen the final demise of the sailing warship, the change from wood to iron and then to steel in ship construction, and major improvements in armaments. HMS *Dreadnought*, launched in 1906, was the culmination of all these technical improvements and at a stroke not only set new standards of warship design, but also fundamentally altered the way battles would in future be fought. The greatly increased accuracy of heavy guns had been amply demonstrated in the Russo-Japanese War of 1904–5, and several navies were planning 'all big-gun' battleships. But as a result of Fisher's persistence, Great Britain's was the first navy to acquire the new type of battleship. By being first in the 'dreadnought race' Britain secured a huge advantage over Germany and by the end of the First World War had completed forty-eight dreadnoughts to the latter's twenty-six. And the dreadnought formula of high speed, heavy armour and all big-gun armament was to remain a standard up to the Second World War, when its vulnerability to air attack introduced yet another element into the equation. Air power and the emergence of the submarine as dominant players in the maritime balance of power introduced yet further levels of technological sophistication which, while their developments were to be twentieth-century phenomena, had their roots firmly in the preceding half-century of astonishing technological advance.

Daguerreotype portrait of a Greenwich pensioner, 1840s

Photographer unknown

Built on the site of the old royal palace at Greenwich, the Royal Hospital was founded as a naval equivalent of the Chelsea Hospital for soldiers. The first pensioners arrived in 1705 and the hospital continued to function until 1869, when it was closed and converted for use as the Royal Naval College. The decision to close the hospital may have been influenced by the behaviour of the pensioners themselves in later years, for, as *Dickens' Dictionary of the Thames* (1893) records, the hospital had become 'one of the sights of London, and it is possible that a too liberal distribution of *baksheesh* on the part of the public may have had something to do with the deterioration which was observable in the manners and customs of the in-pensioners during the latter days of their existence'.

Below: **Pupil at the Royal Hospital School, Greenwich,
c. 1860**

Photographer unknown

The founding of the Royal Hospital had also made provision for
the education of impoverished children for the navy, and in the
nineteenth century the school was housed in the buildings that later
became the National Maritime Museum. A prominent landmark in
the grounds was the ship *Fame*, a full-scale model built in front of
the Queen's House to give the boys practice in working rigging.
The school was transferred to a new site in Suffolk in 1933.

Opposite above: **Classroom at the Royal Hospital School,
Greenwich, 1855**

Photographer unknown

This photograph, from the earliest surviving album of portraits of
staff and pupils at the Royal Hospital School, shows a class in progress in the Queen's House. The master seen here has been identified as John Riddle, who succeeded his father Edward as headmaster
in 1851. John Riddle had joined the staff of the school as an assistant
master at the remarkably early age of fifteen; his period as headmaster was ended, however, when he died in 1862 as a result of
falling from the classroom platform during a lesson.

Opposite below: **Vice-Admiral Sir Henry Keppel KCB
and staff, China Station, 1868**

Photographer unknown

This portrait of Sir Henry Keppel (1809–1904) was taken on board
his flagship HMS *Rodney* during his period as Commander-in-Chief
of the China Station. One of the most distinguished of nineteenth-
century naval officers, Keppel's career spanned the whole Victorian
age: he joined the navy in 1822, saw service in China, Borneo, the
Baltic and South America, and was made Admiral of the Fleet in
1877. In his last years he was an intimate friend of Edward VII.
Other figures in the group are Captain (later Admiral Sir) Algernon
Heneage (seated), the ship's secretary William Fisk (second from
left) and Lieutenant Henry Stephenson.

**The training ship *King Alfred* on the Thames
near Reading, *c.* 1900**

Photograph by Francis Frith & Co.

Several unofficial organizations also catered for maritime enthusiasms, and this photograph shows young cadets posed in front of the brig-rigged *King Alfred*, an unseaworthy-looking vessel that appears to have been constructed on the hull of a Thames lighter.

Workshop at the Britannia Royal Naval College, Dartmouth, _c._ 1912

Photographer unknown

The inadequacies of the officer training ship _Britannia_, which had been moored at Dartmouth since 1863, were fully recognized by the 1870s but it was not until the turn of the century that practical steps were taken to remedy the situation. Much of the impetus for this came from Lord Fisher's determination to create a truly professional modern navy, and in 1901 building work started on the present training college at Dartmouth. The new school for direct-entry officers was opened in 1905.

Below: **Stokers on the turret ship HMS *Edinburgh*, c. 1897**
Photograph by Stuart
Stokers in the Royal Navy at this period were recruited from physically fit men of good character aged between eighteen and twenty-five. No other qualifications were demanded, and after a six- or

seven-month period of training (which included small arms proficiency) they were drafted to naval vessels as second class stokers. Their pay reflected the strenuous nature of their work and was relatively generous for the period, starting at £30 and rising to a maximum of £90 a year for a first class stoker.

Opposite above: **Sailors scrubbing the decks, HMS *Edinburgh*, c. 1888**
Photographer unknown
This picture sums up much of the monotonous routine that was required on board ship, a pattern of work described by Henry Bosanquet in *The Royal Navy* (1897): 'Every morning at the same hour the hands turn out (generally about five o'clock in harbour) and about two-and-a-half hours are devoted to cleaning all parts of

the ship, boats, guns, etc., and getting them into the spick and span condition for which our warships are famous.'

Opposite below: **Sailors relaxing on board the cruiser HMS *Lancaster*, c. 1910**
Photographer unknown
This rare informal view shows sailors relaxing off duty in the heat of the Mediterranean during a commission of HMS *Lancaster*.

Below: **Serving out the grog ration, HMS *Dido*, c. 1910**
Photographer unknown
From 1740 until its abolition in 1970 the issue of the rum ration was a highlight of the sailor's day. A measure of spirits had traditionally been granted to sailors while at sea, but the practice of using a

diluted concoction (three parts water to one part rum) was started on board ships in the West Indies and is attributed to Admiral Edward Vernon (known as 'Old Grog' after his grogram coat). The issue was served at 12.30 each day, each man being entitled to half a pint.

SERVING OUT GROG.

Opposite above: **Armourers at work, HMS *Edinburgh*, 1890s**
Photograph by Stuart
Armourers formed part of the Artisan Branch of the Royal Navy, a section which included blacksmiths, carpenters, coopers, painters and plumbers. They were recruited into the navy from these trades, and their pay, which ranged from £36 to £118 a year, reflected the skilled nature of their calling. This group is posed in front of one of *Edinburgh*'s six-inch breech-loading guns.

Opposite below: **Attaching cable to anchor davit, HMS *Edinburgh*, 1890s**
Photograph by Stuart
Although somewhat formally posed, Stuart's series of views of the various tasks undertaken on board ship provides a valuable record of the many specialized jobs undertaken by seamen in the late nineteenth century.

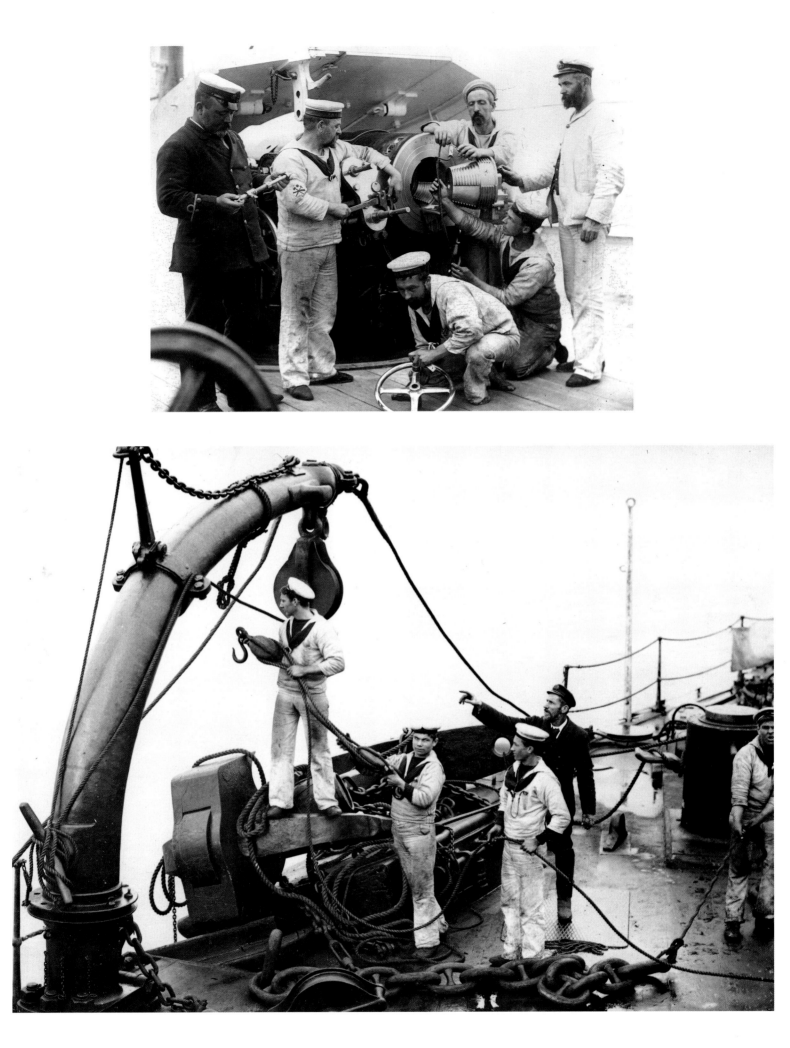

British ships at Balaclava, 1855

Photograph by Roger Fenton

The Russian destruction of the Turkish fleet at Sinope in November 1853 and the sending of British and French warships into the Black Sea to prevent Russian landings resulted in the entry of Britain and France into the Crimean War in March 1854. Roger Fenton, together with his assistants and his famous photographic van, was in Balaclava between March and June 1855, in which time he produced the first extensive series of war photographs.

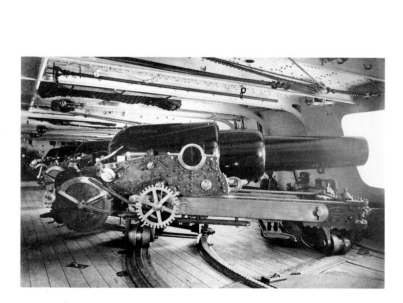

Ten-inch MLR gun in main barbette, HMS *Sultan*, 1870s

Photographer unknown

This photograph gives a vivid impression of the massive increase in the size of naval armaments in the decades after the Crimean War. At 9,290 tons, HMS *Sultan* was one of the largest of the central battery ships. She was completed at Chatham in 1871 and carried eight ten-inch and four nine-inch muzzle-loading rifled guns in a two-tiered battery fitted with embrasures. The gun seen here was situated in a barbette built out from the side of the ship to increase the arc of fire.

Left: **HMS *Iris* in dry dock, Malta,** *c.* **1880**
Photographer unknown
The Iris class dispatch vessels were the first Royal Naval warships to be constructed of steel. With her elegant clipper bow, *Iris* was designed for high speed at the expense of heavy armament and protective armour. She attained a speed of nearly eighteen knots during trials, and with her sister ship HMS *Mercury* was the fastest warship in existence at the time of her completion.

Below: **The launch of HMS *Melita* at Malta, 1888**
Photographer unknown
Seen here amid a festive fleet of *dghaisas*, HMS *Melita* slides off the stocks at the Malta Dockyard on 20 March 1888. One of six Mariner class composite screw sloops, she was the only one of her type to be built at Malta. This decision was made to give employment on the island, although construction costs were about 20 per cent higher than in the Royal Dockyards. In 1905 she was converted to a boom defence vessel and later became a salvage vessel before being sold to the Falmouth Docks Board in 1920.

HMS *Polyphemus* fitting out at Chatham, 1881–2

Photographer unknown

HMS *Polyphemus* was one of the first generation of Royal Naval vessels armed with broadside torpedoes. She is more famous, however, for her unique ram bow, a massive ten-foot projection designed as a secondary means of attack. Lightly armed, highly manoeuvrable and with the then phenomenal speed of eighteen knots, she was intended for swift and deadly attack on enemy battleships. Although the ram was successful in trials, *Polyphemus* was never tested in action and was finally broken up in 1903.

QUARTER DECK H.M.S RODNEY 9635 STUART COPYRIGHT
W GREGORY & Co 51 STRAND LONDON

HMS *Rodney* and Thames barge, *c.* 1900
Photographer unknown
In a photograph skilfully contrasting two very different aspects of maritime life, a Thames barge sails past the massive thirteen-and-a-half-inch guns of the second class barbette ship *Rodney* (launched 1884).

Opposite: **Repairs to the bows of HMS *Hawke*, September 1911**
Photographer unknown
Launched in 1891, HMS *Hawke* was one of the nine Edgar class protected cruisers built under the provisions of the Naval Defence Act of 1889. This close-up view of her bows shows her in dry dock in Portsmouth after being damaged in a collision with the liner *Olympic* off Southampton on 20 September 1911. She was given a straight bow after the accident. Although obsolete by 1914, this class saw a good deal of service in the First World War. HMS *Hawke* was an early casualty, however, being torpedoed by a German U-boat on 15 October 1914 with a loss of 524 lives.

Right: **Construction of the new dockyard at Gibraltar: Dock No. 1, 24 May 1904**

Photographer unknown

As British imperial responsibilities grew, the facilities provided by many naval bases proved insufficient and the early twentieth century saw dockyard improvements put into effect in several of the colonial dependencies. Construction of three new moles and the dredging of the harbour at Gibraltar to accommodate modern battleships was one of the largest of these projects, and was followed in 1903–6 by the building of three graving docks on forty-seven acres of reclaimed land.

The Old Mole, Gibraltar, 1864

Photographer unknown

Seen at their moorings in the harbour at Gibraltar before the extensive works of the twentieth century are two of the early ironclad battleships, HMS *Resistance* (completed in 1862) and, behind her, HMS *Royal Oak*, completed in 1863 and the first British ironclad to enter the Mediterranean.

**HMS *Dreadnought* under construction, Portsmouth,
5 October 1905**

Photographer unknown

This view shows the frames of HMS *Dreadnought* shortly after the start of construction. The first of the 'all big gun' battleships and a product of Lord Fisher's determined modernization of the Royal Navy, her many innovative features were destined to make her the model to which navies all over the world subsequently aspired. Fisher and his colleagues had correctly predicted massive increases in the range at which sea battles would be fought in the twentieth century, and effective fire control at this range demanded the uniformity and power of armament supplied by *Dreadnought*'s twelve-inch guns. She was also the first battleship to be fitted with turbine engines, which delivered high speed, light weight and economy of maintenance.

HMS *Dreadnought*, Portsmouth, 2 June 1906
Photographer unknown
In an astonishing feat of shipbuilding never since equalled, *Dreadnought* was constructed at high speed and in great secrecy: she was launched in February 1906 and ran her first trials in December of that year, little over twelve months after the laying of her first keel plates. Superior in speed and firepower to all other capital ships then afloat, she immediately set a standard of warship design which survived largely unchanged in essentials until the Second World War. *Dreadnought* served in the Grand Fleet for the first half of the First World War, and in March 1915 rammed and sank *U29* in the North Sea. She was sold for breaking up in 1920.

HMS *Hindustan* leading the Third Battle Squadron, 1909
Photographer unknown
HMS *Hindustan* (1903) is seen in heavy seas ahead of HMS *Africa* (1905) and HMS *Dominion* (1903). These King Edward VII class battleships were the immediate predecessors of the revolutionary *Dreadnought* and were the last ships to be built to the designs of the distinguished naval architect Sir William White.

Turbinia under way, _c._ 1900
Photographer unknown
The _Turbinia,_ designed by Sir Charles Parsons and the first vessel in the world to be powered by steam turbines, made a sensational first appearance at the Diamond Jubilee Naval Review of 1897, attaining a hitherto unheard-of speed of thirty knots and attracting massive publicity. The introduction of turbine engines in ships of all types swiftly followed, notably in HMS _Dreadnought_ in 1905.

'B' and 'C' Class submarines at HMS _Dolphin_, Gosport, 1909
Photograph by E. Hopkins
The British Admiralty was forced to abandon its initial hostility to submarines at the start of the twentieth century in response to American and French investment in this new form of warfare. By 1903 five 'Holland' class submarines were in service, and by 1906

the Admiralty felt sufficient confidence in its grasp of the new technology to order a production run of thirty-eight 'C' Class submarines. Ultimately, the small 'coastal' design of these submarines delayed the introduction of proper overseas patrol submarines, but even so many of them saw continuous service throughout the First World War.

***U155* at Tower Bridge, London, 1919**
Photographer unknown
U155, launched in 1916 as the *Deutschland*, was one of only two cargo submarines built in the First World War. She made two voyages to America in a mercantile capacity before being taken over and armed by the German navy in February 1917. She was surrendered to the British in November 1918 and in the following year she was placed on display as a floating exhibition at Temple Pier in London.

TO THE ENDS OF THE EARTH

Lookout on a whaling ship, 1900s
Photographer unknown

The end of the Napoleonic Wars in 1815 ushered in an era of peace for the Royal Navy which, apart from periodic colonial disturbances and the larger Crimean conflagration of the 1850s, persisted unbroken until the First World War. For ambitious young naval officers peace was the most effective destroyer of careers, slowing the pace of promotion and consigning the energies of a generation of officers to the tedious policing of the trade routes, enlivened only by the prospect perhaps of chasing pirates in China or slavers off the coast of Africa. New avenues to glory were needed; as the veteran explorer Sherard Osborn robustly observed: 'The Navy needs some action to wake it from the sloth of routine and save it from the canker of prolonged peace . . .'

In succeeding years much energy was to be devoted to the peacetime pursuits of exploration and surveying, particularly of the as yet largely uncharted Arctic regions. Great stress was laid on the scientific aspects of these ventures, while the commercial potential of a north-west passage to the Pacific was a further justification for sending naval expeditions further and further north into the lands of eternal ice. With each succeeding attempt the character of these expeditions changed, and as the goal of a north-west passage receded, it was replaced by a race to the Pole. Patriotic sentiment was shamelessly orchestrated by the press until scientific goals slipped lower and lower down the agenda, ousted by a jingoistic determination to plant the British flag at the top of the world.

Attempts by northern Europeans to discover a shorter route to the Pacific by way of the Arctic Circle had their first impetus in the sixteenth century in the face of Spanish and Portuguese control of the known sea routes to the east. The first voyagers who sailed in search of a north-east passage in the mid sixteenth century discovered a new source of trade in Muscovy and the original inspiration of the voyages was largely forgotten. Thenceforward the search for a route to the east was concentrated on a possible north-west passage across the roof of the North American landmass. This too

Opposite: **Ice mountain called the Sugar Loaf, Antarctica, 1911**
Photograph by Herbert Ponting

157

led to new commercial opportunities with the opening up of the great fur-trading lands surrounding Hudson's Bay. By the mid eighteenth century the existence of such a passage was becoming debatable, and although Captain Cook's entry into the Arctic Sea through the Bering Strait in 1778 indicated a possible route into the Pacific, entry to the passage from the North Atlantic eluded discovery and interest waned until the nineteenth century, by which time the Arctic coast of mainland North America was fairly well explored.

Naval expeditions to investigate the possibility that the North Pole might lie in the centre of a temperate sea had been sent out sporadically in the late eighteenth century, but a new age of Arctic exploration was ushered in as a result of the scientific observations and descriptions made by the whaling captain William Scoresby. His report that the Arctic was less ice-bound than in former years re-awakened interest in the search for a north-west passage, and from 1818 a series of exploratory naval expeditions was sent to the northern seas. In that year vessels under the command of John Ross and Edward Parry investigated a route through Baffin Bay, while David Buchan and John Franklin pushed north into the Greenland Sea until defeated by ice. The following twenty-five years saw a succession of voyages which slowly opened out the frontiers of Arctic knowledge in the form of mapping and the collection of scientific data. For some the chance of glory and immortality among the pantheon of explorers was the driving force; for others the attraction of the substantial rewards offered by the government for discovery of the north-west passage was the motive; while for John Ross, further expeditions were the chance to salvage a reputation damaged by his sighting of a range of mountains that later proved non-existent.

In 1845 the most famous of all Arctic expeditions set out in an attempt to resolve finally the question of a north-west passage. Two years later no news had been heard of Sir John Franklin's ships, HMS *Erebus* and HMS *Terror*, and in 1848 the first of a series of expeditions – some organized by the government, some by Franklin's widow – was sent out to discover his fate. The mystery was resolved by the *Fox* expedition of 1857–9, which found the cairn on King William Island telling of Franklin's death a decade before.

The Franklin tragedy turned the Admiralty against Arctic exploration, and it was only the ceaseless lobbying of Clements Markham and Sherard Osborn that finally persuaded the Admiralty to mount a new attempt on the Pole. Pouring scorn on those who criticized any new attempt (and implicitly questioning both their patriotism and their courage),

these two distinguished explorers raised the unthinkable spectre of a nation other than Great Britain being first to the North Pole. This was enough to turn the tide of public opinion, and huge crowds gathered at Portsmouth on 29 May 1875 to cheer as HMS *Discovery* and HMS *Alert* set sail under the command of Captain (later Sir) George Nares. The goal had now changed, and no longer did the search for a north-west passage figure prominently on the agenda: '. . . the scope and primary object of the Expedition should be to attain the highest Northern latitude, and, if possible, to reach the North Pole . . .'

The expedition proved to be – like the Franklin Expedition before it – a prime example of brave men blundering amateurishly and ill-prepared into regions whose full perils they failed to appreciate. The advice of the expert John Rae, who advocated snowshoes and the building of snowhouses rather than transporting heavy canvas tents, was largely ignored, as was sound information on the best clothing. Little training was given in the control of dog teams, and the rations were entirely inadequate for the immensely heavy work the men were called upon to undertake.

Leaving the *Discovery* to set up permanent winter quarters in Lady Franklin Bay, Nares took the *Alert* north, edging round Ellesmere Island until, at the end of August, he found a bay where he could winter safely on the edge of the Polar Sea. Despite Nares's own conviction that the Pole could not be reached, he had his orders and the following months were spent in a gruelling series of trips to lay out depots for an attempt on the Pole the following spring. On 3 April 1876 two sledging expeditions were sent out from the *Alert*, but within a few days the first signs of scurvy began to appear. On 24 April Albert Markham's teams had reached the 83rd parallel of latitude – the furthest north a white man had thus far gone – but his crew had also reached the limit of their endurance. Markham was forced to turn back, still some 400 nautical miles from the Pole and unaware that the route he had taken contained the most ridged and difficult ice of the whole Arctic Ocean. Markham's team was finally rescued by a team sent out from the *Alert*, while a further team from *Discovery*, under the leadership of Lewis Beaumont, also had to be rescued. Nares was expected to remain in the Arctic until 1877, but such was the condition of his men that he realized nothing further could be accomplished, and in July he turned south and returned to England. It was not until 1909 that the American Robert Peary became the first white man to reach the North Pole, after a series of expeditions starting in 1886.

The Nares Expedition was the last traditional Arctic expedition sent out by the navy in the nineteenth century. The expedition had brought back valuable scientific data and had established British sovereignty over Ellesmere Island. But in the public mind it was adjudged a failure and the obloquy naturally fell on Nares, who was accused of lack of determination in pursuit of his goal and who in the subsequent public inquiry into the causes of scurvy was blamed for not taking fresh lime juice (which the navy's medical department had not in fact recommended). Given his situation, Nares's command of the expedition had been exemplary, and he may well have wished that he had not been transferred from his command of HMS *Challenger* to lead this ill-fated journey. For while Nares was imprisoned in the Arctic fastness, his previous command was in the final stages of a hugely successful world cruise whose results were to establish the credentials of oceanography as a science.

Attempts to make deep-sea soundings and to measure the temperature and currents of the oceans had been started in earnest by members of the Royal Society in the late seventeenth century, but it was not until the nineteenth century (after the first Hydrographer to the Navy had been appointed in 1795) that the new science became fully established. Partly this was due to a series of exploring expeditions during which oceanographic observations were made, but it was also a response to the increasing importance of commercial shipping and the laying of submarine telegraphs, both of which demanded a fuller knowledge of the ocean and the seabed. The intellectual demands of the age also played their part, for with the publication of Darwin's *Origin of Species* in 1859, the seas of the world were increasingly looked to as a source of the 'living fossils' which played a part in the evolution debate. In 1868 Charles Wyville Thomson of Edinburgh University persuaded the Royal Navy to lend HMS *Lightning* for a short summer survey cruise in the waters between the Shetlands and the Faroes. This first cruise was of limited practical success due to bad weather and the ship's own shortcomings, but abundant life was found at depths of more than 600 fathoms, and it was verified that the sea's temperature beyond a certain depth did not vary with latitude, as had been previously believed, but that great bodies of water, each keeping its own temperature, were in constant movement beneath the surface. In 1869 the Admiralty loaned a better vessel, HMS *Porcupine*, and a period of dredging some 200 miles west of Ushant confirmed the existence of varied life forms at depths of 2,000 fathoms or more, thus upsetting traditional theories of submarine life.

In 1870 Thomson became Professor of Natural History at Edinburgh University and from this position, and with the experience of these earlier surveys behind him, was able to persuade the Royal Society to approach the Admiralty again with a request for a vessel to undertake a much more ambitious voyage of oceanographic exploration. This application was granted and, with further subsidies granted by William Gladstone's government, preparations for the voyage were put in hand. This far-sighted use of naval craft and personnel resulted in a cruise which was to justify itself not only in the wealth of scientific material with which it returned, but in the impetus it gave to the international scientific community to mount similar investigative expeditions.

HMS *Challenger*, a three-masted ship of 2,300 tons with auxiliary steam power, was fitted out with laboratories and workrooms, and under Thomson's leadership a civilian staff of six undertook the scientific work of a voyage which in the course of its four-year commission was to amass a huge collection of specimens and data both on the structure and behaviour of the oceans and the biology of the marine environment. Among the civilian staff serving under Thomson were the scientist Henry Nottidge Moseley (later Linacre Professor of Human and Comparative Anatomy at Oxford), J.J. Wild, the official artist, John Young Buchanan, chemist and physicist, and a young man of mixed Scottish and Canadian background, a former medical student turned marine scientist named John Murray. Murray was recruited at the last moment to replace a member of the team who dropped out, but in the event it was he who was largely responsible for the most enduring monument of the expedition.

HMS *Challenger* left Portsmouth on 21 December 1872, and after visiting Portugal and Tenerife crossed the Atlantic to the Caribbean before heading south for Cape Town (reached in October 1873). Seven pleasant weeks were spent at the Cape in preparation for the harsher waters of the Southern Ocean, and in mid December 1873 *Challenger* steamed south to Kerguelen Island and on to the drifting icefields of the Antarctic Circle. From here a course was set north-east to Melbourne and Sydney, and then via New Zealand and Cape York up through the islands of the Philippines to Hong Kong. *Challenger* then retraced her route as far south as the northern coast of New Guinea before striking north to Japan and then on to the islands of the Pacific. Valparaiso was visited in November 1875, and after sailing through the Straits of Magellan in the first days of January 1876, *Challenger* visited the Falkland Islands and Montevideo before heading for England, where she arrived at Spithead on

24 May 1876. Such a bald summary does scant justice to the immense labours undertaken by the ship's company in the course of the voyage.

During their four years at sea the scientists had amassed a vast collection of material that was to keep specialists in various fields occupied for years to come. In a voyage of nearly 70,000 nautical miles 362 observing stations were set up and at each of these a standard procedure was carried out: the depth was determined, samples of water and of the ocean floor were taken, the temperature was measured, meteorological observations were made, and currents were evaluated. Much of this work, valuable as it was to prove, was dull and repetitive, involving heavy work in often adverse weather. The basic scientific tool of the *Challenger* was the dredge – very similar to a fishing trawl – by means of which samples were brought up from the ocean floor or from intermediate levels. This generally tedious and sometimes dangerous work was continued throughout the cruise, and by its end huge amounts of material, including a mass of formerly unknown marine creatures, had been recovered from all parts of the globe, the raw data for a generation of specialists. But the scientists of HMS *Challenger* did not restrict themselves to the generally minute fauna and flora of the deep. Parties were sent ashore at each anchorage to observe and collect animal and botanical specimens, and in addition to their rigorous scientific work many of the civilian staff produced charming sketches and descriptions of the places visited. Observations were also made of the many human cultures through which they passed, and photographs either taken or purchased of various ethnic groups. Among the various adventures and social events of the cruise were the rescuing of two German whalers who had been stranded on Inaccessible Island (near Tristan da Cunha) for two years, encounters with Fiji cannibals in the penal settlement at Ovalau Island, and a visit from King Kalakaua of Hawaii, who proved a cultivated man, much interested in the work of the expedition.

The true monument to this major scientific achievement, however, did not appear for another decade and more, and was to owe its completion largely to the persistence of John Murray, who took over the editorship of the official report when Sir Charles Wyville Thomson died in March 1882. His labours were prodigious and in 1895, when the project was completed, the scientific report of the *Challenger* Expedition amounted to fifty massive volumes, of which seven were written exclusively or largely by Murray himself. By this time the Treasury had long since ceased to fund the work, and the final volumes of 'the greatest advance in the knowledge of our planet since the celebrated geographical discoveries of the fifteenth and sixteenth centuries' were completed at Murray's own expense.

The navigators and explorers of northern Europe came to the great frozen continent of Antarctica far later than to the Arctic. Captain Cook in 1773 was the first man to circumnavigate Antarctica, and following the publication of his *Voyage*, seal hunters entered the Southern Ocean. It was not, however, until the 1820s and 30s (by which time Arctic exploration, fuelled by the possibilities of a north-west passage, was getting into its stride) that exploration of the coastline of Antarctica got fully under way, and the first indisputable sighting of land in Greater Antarctica was made by Captain John Biscoe in the *Tula* in February 1831. This was followed by three national expeditions – French, American and British – which between 1837 and 1843 started the charting of the Antarctic coastline. The British expedition was led by Captain James Clark Ross, already a veteran of Arctic exploration, who in 1839–43 took the *Terror* and the *Erebus* past the ice barrier guarding the Ross Sea and up to the great wall of ice known as the Ross Ice Shelf. After these pioneering efforts, Antarctic exploration waned for nearly half a century, with the exception of the brief visit of HMS *Challenger* to southern waters. Interest picked up again in the closing years of the nineteenth century, particularly after the Sixth International Geographical Congress of 1895 urged the scientific community to give priority to the Antarctic, and a number of scientific expeditions again started to investigate the fringes of the icebound continent. With the new century came what is generally known as the 'heroic' period of Antarctic exploration, as patriotic fervour again sent some of the world's finest explorers in what was to become a race for the Pole.

Robert Falcon Scott was recommended for the command of the National Antarctic Expedition by that tireless lobbyist for British exploration Sir Clements Markham, and in August 1901 he sailed in command of the research ship *Discovery*, with the scientific exploration of Victoria Land on the edge of the Ross Sea, as his objective. The party wintered at Hut Point, McMurdo Sound, beneath the smoking plume of Mount Erebus, and in addition to carrying out a full scientific programme in the area made the first extensive land explorations of the Antarctic, reaching beyond 82° South and tracing the range of mountains beyond the Ross Ice Shelf. In the following season, they penetrated the great ice plateau that covers the centre of the continent.

The pace of exploration quickened in the following years: Ernest Shackleton's team came to within 100 miles of the

Pole during the British Antarctic Expedition of 1907–9, and in that year Scott was chosen to head a second expedition in the Dundee whaler *Terra Nova*, which had acted as one of the relief ships during the *Discovery* expedition. While scientific objectives were theoretically to the fore, it was the possibility of reaching the South Pole that produced the financial sponsorship necessary to fund the journey. By early December 1910 the *Terra Nova* was battling through the pack ice, and by the end of that month she had reached the open waters of the Ross Sea. By the end of January 1911 the party was settled into its quarters at Cape Evans at the foot of Mount Erebus, and for the next months they worked through the Antarctic winter, exercising and making scientific observations. The sun returned towards the end of August, and two months later, on 1 November 1911, the two main parties left for the assault on the Pole.

The end of the story is one of the great tragedies of modern exploration. On 4 January 1912, Scott, E.A. Wilson, L.E.G. Oates, Edgar Evans and H.R. Bowers set off for the final 150-mile march to the Pole, arriving on 17 January 1912 with the bitter knowledge that the Norwegian Amundsen had beaten them by a month. The return journey was unremitting nightmare, as the weather closed and the party grew weaker by the day. The final marches, as fuel and rations started to run out, progress became slower and slower, and frostbite took hold, make painful reading in Scott's last diary entries. The final note, dated 29 March 1912, acknowledges the inevitability of their end, only ten miles from the next food depot. Eight months later, in the following November, their bodies were found and a cairn raised above their final resting place. Arguments about the relative professionalism of Scott against Amundsen have raged ever since, but no one would contradict the appositeness of the quotation from Tennyson's *Ulysses* inscribed on the cross which overlooks the Great Ice Barrier: 'To strive, to seek, to find and not to yield.'

The three expeditions illustrated in this chapter span the globe and cover a period of three decades, but photography forms a unifying feature, since in all three the medium played an important role both as an instrument of record and as a powerful artistic account of discovery and exploration. Since the early days of photography the possible use of the medium had been discussed as an aid to explorers, but the difficulties and uncertainties of early attempts resulted in little distinguished work up to the 1860s. But in the late 1850s the Royal Engineers had started to teach photography as part of their curriculum, and their expertise led to a wider use of the camera under the difficult circumstances that expedition work imposed.

The first official photographer on board HMS *Challenger* was a corporal seconded from the Royal Engineers, although he deserted at Cape Town and had to be replaced. Similarly, for photographic work on the Nares Arctic Expedition, Thomas Mitchell, paymaster of HMS *Discovery*, and George White, assistant engineer on HMS *Alert*, were instructed in photography by the Royal Engineers at Chatham. Given the short notice at which this was carried out, they produced very commendable results which were later marketed commercially by the London Stereoscopic Company. The photographer accompanying Scott's last voyage to the Antarctic was the finest artist of all. Already an established travel photographer and pioneer cinematographer when he was appointed official photographer, Herbert Ponting produced not only a fine factual record of the expedition and its members, but also made some of the most hauntingly beautiful images of those majestic wastes of snow and ice (an achievement all the more remarkable given the notorious technical difficulties of photographing such subjects). His skills were fully appreciated by Scott himself, who wrote a perceptive account of Ponting's work in his diary entry in April 1911:

> Of the many admirable points in this work, perhaps the most notable are Ponting's eye for a picture and the mastery he has acquired of ice subjects; the composition of most of his pictures is extraordinarily good, he seems to know by instinct the exact value of foreground and middle distance and of the introduction of 'life', whilst with more technical skill in the manipulation of screens [i.e. filters] and exposures, he emphasizes the subtle shadows of the snow and reproduces its wondrously transparent texture. He is an artist in love with his work . . .

**Men from *Alert* cutting ice blocks in Dobbin Bay,
August 1875**

Photograph by Thomas Mitchell or George White

Dobbin Bay, on the eastward side of the massive promontory of
Cape Hawks on Ellesmere Island, was a rendezvous point for *Alert*
and *Discovery*. Here men from *Alert* can be seen using sheerlegs to
raise blocks of ice for melting down and use on board ship.

Above: **Group on board *Alert*, 1875**

Photograph by Thomas Mitchell or George White

The bearded figure of the expedition's commander, Captain George Strong Nares, stands in the centre of this group, photographed at the start of the voyage. Standing to Nares's right is Lieutenant William May, a future Admiral of the Fleet. Standing on Nares's left is Lieutenant Pelham Aldrich, who was to lead a gruelling sledge party round the northern tip of Ellesmere Island. Commander Albert Markham, leader of the sledge party that reached latitude 83°20' in early 1876, is the bearded figure seated immediately in front of the chimney pipe.

Right: **Walrus killed by *Alert* at Cape Prescott, August 1875**

Photograph by Thomas Mitchell or George White

This is the twelve-and-a-half-foot walrus harpooned by Commander Albert Markham and brought back to the ship. The flesh and blubber from the unfortunate animal filled five 250 lb casks, while 'the meat when fried was much appreciated by all of us, and the liver was pronounced to be excellent. The dogs made a hearty meal off the scraps.'

**Eskimo dog driver Hans Hendrik and family,
on board *Discovery*, July 1875**

Photograph by Thomas Mitchell or George White

The Greenland Eskimo Hans Hendrik was a dog handler whose immense Arctic experience included service with the American expeditions of Elisha Kane in 1853–5, Isaac Hayes in 1860–61 and Charles Hall's disastrous *Polaris* expedition of 1871–3. It was Hendrik and his dog team who were largely responsible for rescuing Lieutenant Lewis Beaumont's *Discovery* sledging party in June 1876. He is seen here with his wife Merkut and their son.

***Opposite below:* Shipkeepers and seedy dogs
in front of *Discovery*, April 1876**

Photograph by Thomas Mitchell or George White

Despite taking fifty-five Greenland dogs and their Eskimo handlers on the expedition, Nares remained unconvinced of their usefulness. The insistence on using men to drag the heavy loads was a major factor in the hardships experienced by the sledge teams sent out from *Alert* and *Discovery* and contributed to the deaths that resulted. The condition of the dogs seen here is explained by a mystery disease that killed many of them, and by the winter's inactivity, which left them unexercised when spring came.

Above: Pemmican blocks on the deck of *Alert*, 1875

Photograph by Thomas Mitchell or George White

The carbohydrate-rich qualities of pemmican were considered a valuable 'heat-giving' food source for Arctic explorers. Opinions as to its culinary qualities were more mixed, although Nares states that the pemmican biscuits given to the sledge crews were much liked. An Indian invention, this preserved food, which could last for several years, was made from strips of beef ground up and mixed with an equal quantity of fat. Currants and other extras were sometimes added by Arctic travellers.

Right: **J. J. Wild, artist, sketching Royal Sound, Kerguelen Island, January 1874**

Challenger *photographer*

Wild, the official artist to the expedition, was of Swiss nationality and later wrote an account of the voyage entitled *At Anchor* (1878). He was one of the most productive members of *Challenger*'s staff, producing a wealth of scientific drawings and landscape views with which the final report was illustrated. He is here seen wearing the Antarctic clothing issued to expedition members.

Below: **Group from HMS *Challenger* skinning penguins, Inaccessible Island, 1873**

Challenger *photographer*

It is unclear whether the group seen here are skinning penguins as specimens for preservation, or for food. Spry records that although penguin soup was prepared during the voyage (on the recommendation of the polar explorer Sir James Ross, who considered it comparable to hare soup), none of the party could bring themselves to sample it.

HMS *Challenger* in dry dock at Yokosuka, 1875
Challenger *photographer*
After a tedious voyage from the Philippines, the weeks spent in Japan proved a period of much-needed relaxation and recuperation.

Advantage was also taken of the modern docking facilities in the government arsenal at Yokosuka, and here *Challenger* spent a week in dry dock while her rudder was repaired and a general overhaul carried out.

Opposite above: **Mic-Mac Indians, Nova Scotia, Canada, May 1873**

Challenger *photographer*

The scientists aboard *Challenger* took particular interest in the societies and varied racial types encountered during the voyage, and this is one of many ethnographical studies taken by the official photographer.

Opposite below: **Gold mine near Halifax, Nova Scotia, Canada, May 1873**

Challenger *photographer*

Wyville Thomson thought Halifax like 'a second-rate English seaport, with its dull streets of square houses blackened with coal smoke', when *Challenger* visited Nova Scotia. Interesting excursions were made, however, to the gold mines near Dartmouth where, 'in a wild, bleak piece of country . . . a small but tolerably certain' yield of gold was extracted.

Above: **Dobo, chief port of the Aru Islands, September 1875**

Challenger *photographer*

The Aru Islands, situated 'quite out of the track of all European trade' off the south-west coast of New Guinea, were a part of the Dutch East Indies at this period. The group was visited by *Challenger* between 16 and 23 September 1875, and at Dobo they were welcomed by 'Malay officials in their gay and pretty state dresses'. Here a happy week was spent searching for ornithological specimens, particularly the beautiful bird of paradise or ribbontail.

Right: **The *Terra Nova* in winter quarters, Cape Evans, 1911**
Photograph by Herbert Ponting

The dramatic perspective seen in this picture emphasizes the immense strength of the Antarctic ice. The *Terra Nova*, built in 1884, was no stranger to such conditions, having served in the Jackson–Harmsworth Arctic Expedition of 1894–7, as well as accompanying the *Morning* in the relief of Scott's earlier Antarctic expedition. She survived Scott's 1910–13 expedition and was engaged in the Newfoundland seal trade and later as a coastal trader until 1943.

The *Terra Nova* in winter quarters, Cape Evans, 1911
Photograph by Herbert Ponting

This photograph shows the *Terra Nova* raised up and heeling over in her winter quarters in McMurdo Sound after the expedition's arrival at the base camp. It again vividly illustrates the power of natural forces in the Antarctic, but as one of the sturdiest of the old Scottish whalers, the *Terra Nova* was built to withstand such punishment.

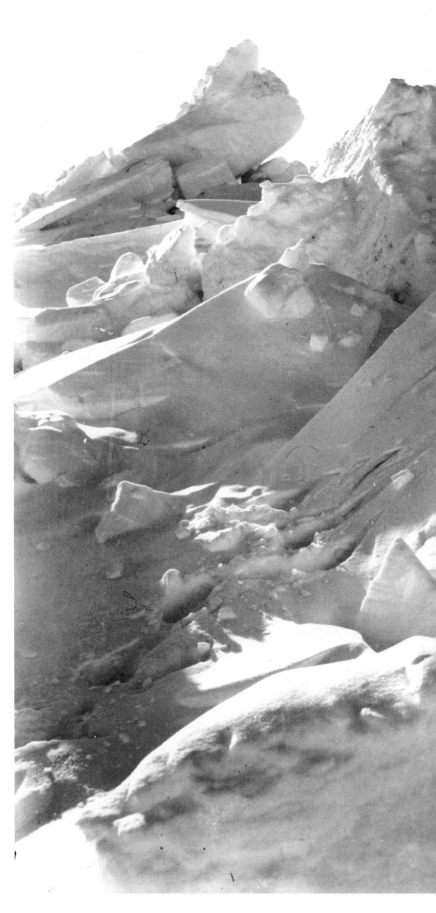

Right: **The *Terra Nova* in a storm in the Southern Ocean, late November 1910**

Photograph by Herbert Ponting

Although he suffered badly from seasickness during the journey to the Antarctic, Ponting continued to take photographs (once very nearly losing his finest camera), and this dramatic view shows the pumps being manned during a gale. On 2 December, a few days after this photograph was taken, two ponies and a dog died and ten tons of coal had to be thrown overboard in the course of the most violent storm of the voyage.

Below: **The wardroom of the *Terra Nova*, 1910**

Photograph by Herbert Ponting

This group portrait shows the officers and scientists of Scott's expedition in the wardroom of the *Terra Nova* during the voyage to the Antarctic. Captain Scott is seated at the head of the table in the background. Standing, second from the right, is Captain Oates, who was in charge of the ponies during the expedition and who died during the return from the Pole.

The ice-pack from the main-top of the *Terra Nova*, 22 December 1910

Photograph by Herbert Ponting

The *Terra Nova* encountered the first pack ice on her journey to Antarctica on 9 December. From then until 30 December the ship struggled through the ice, consuming over 60 tons of precious coal before she reached the open waters of the Ross Sea. The figures on the yard are, from right to left, the Norwegian skiing expert Tryggve Gran, the Australian geologist T. Griffith Taylor, and the physicist C.S. Wright.

Above: **Base camp at Cape Evans, with Mount Erebus in the background, January 1911**

Photograph by Herbert Ponting

Photographed in early January, about a week after the party's arrival, this scene shows the camp during the landing of stores and the assembling of the living quarters that were to serve as the expedition's base for the next year. By 19 January, in the midst of this harsh environment, Scott was able to write in his diary: 'The hut is becoming the most comfortable dwelling place imaginable . . . a truly seductive home . . . the finest that has ever been erected in the Polar regions.'

Right: **Captain Scott, 13 April 1911**

Photograph by Herbert Ponting

This portrait of Scott was taken on his return to Cape Evans from the old *Discovery* hut, where a party had been setting up the main forward depot for the assault on the South Pole. Already misfortune was starting to dog the expedition: several ponies were lost, and owing to bad weather they were unable to ferry the supplies as far south as had originally been hoped. An additional bad omen was the news of Amundsen's successful landing, with his dogs, at a point sixty miles nearer the Pole.

Opposite: **The Grotto Berg, Antarctica, 5 January 1911**

Photograph by Herbert Ponting

The figure posed in front of the ice cave is the geologist T. Griffith Taylor (1880–1964), whose account of the expedition, *With Scott: The Silver Lining*, was published in 1915.

VALEDICTION

ALAN VILLIERS AND THE LAST DAYS OF SAIL

Accordion player on board the *Parma*, 1932–3
Photograph by Alan Villiers

In his autobiography, *The Set of the Sails*, Alan Villiers describes how the sea impinged on his infant consciousness from his very earliest days. For a man whose whole life was to be devoted to the sailing ship in all its forms, the winds and seas of the southern hemisphere form a suitably romantic and storm-tossed backdrop:

> The equinoctial gales howled about the little weather-board house and roared through the riggings of the square-rigged ships at the bottom of our street, on the night when I was born. It was September 23 1903.

Early infected by the magic of the sea, Villiers, despite his parents' and later his first wife's opposition, never succeeded in struggling for long against its irresistible call. His forebears on his mother's side had come to Australia in the great gold-rush days of the 1850s, while his father, after twelve years spent pioneering in the bush, had taken a poorly paid job as a gripman on the Melbourne tramway system. Academic qualifications and a steady job were their ambitions for their son, but days spent roaming the docks of Melbourne in the years before the First World War merely served to feed a yearning for the sea that his parents were powerless to divert into safer channels.

The deep-sea sailing ship was still at this time a vessel of importance in international trade, as the last generation of great square-riggers fought off the steamship's challenge for the transport of bulk cargoes like wheat from Australia to Europe. And Villiers's earliest memories of his youth were of gazing at these ships in wonder and admiration, noting down details of their rigging and sketching their form. These days spent wandering the Melbourne docks with his brother Frank resulted in a precocious knowledge of the technicalities of maritime life, although this was a knowledge hopelessly imbued with a romantic vision of the sea culled from the writings of novelists like Marryat. At the age of eleven he attempted to sign on to the Norwegian barque *Hippen*, but was dissuaded from running away to sea by the mate with the soundly practical advice: 'Don't let the books fool you,

Opposite: **Topgallant sails being changed on the *Parma*, 1933**
Photograph by Alan Villiers

177

my boy. There's no sailor writing them.' Needless to say, such words made little impression, and his father's attempt to put him off by bringing a former Cape Horner home for supper with tales of hardship at sea was equally unsuccessful. Inspired by the boy's interest and admiration, he stayed for hours, entrancing the young Villiers with tales of hardship, danger and the comradeship of the seafarer's life.

On the death of his father in 1918 Villiers enrolled in a Melbourne sail training school and in 1919, at the age of fifteen, he secured a place as a cadet on the barque *Rothesay Bay*, an aged ship employed in the timber trade between New Zealand and Australia. To Villiers, however, she was 'the very embodiment of romance and sea adventure'. The romance was soon dissipated in ferocious seasickness and the unfriendliness of a drunken crew commanded by a captain sick with cancer. But if this superficial attraction waned, deeper and more lasting bonds were formed: the ties of comradeship and self-reliance in the little world of the ship, together with the sense of a tradition handed down over centuries, known only to seafarers and hidden from lesser mortals on shore – 'the brave spirit of seafaring man'. And the power of this tradition was compounded for Villiers by the knowledge that it was rapidly disappearing. 'Learn all you can,' advised the mate of the *Rothesay Bay*, 'because they'll soon be gone'; and in his next ship, the iron barque *James Craig*, he 'kept something of a log, for I knew that I was sailing at the end of an era'.

The *James Craig* was withdrawn from service for hulking and Villiers, still needing sailing time to earn his ticket, joined the four-masted *Bellands* for a voyage carrying grain to England. Here he learned the full unhappiness of sailing in an English ship, where the rigid division between officers and crew exacerbated the problems of low morale, poor food and a slow passage of 151 days. The *Bellands* arrived in England in 1921 in the depths of a recession and Villiers, after many months searching for a ship, was forced to tramp to Bordeaux before finding a berth on the *Lawhill*, 'a clumsy box of a ship' owned by Captain Gustaf Erikson, the legendary Åland Islander who was among the last of the shipowners to run a profitable business in deep-water sailing ships. Using small, almost skeleton crews of young Åland Islanders who were paid the lowest possible wages, he succeeded in keeping a fleet of vessels in profitable commission. Despite Erikson's practice at that time of recruiting only from his own countrymen, Villiers managed to secure a berth on the *Lawhill* and found her, much to his surprise, to be a happy ship. The smallness of the crew was made up for by labour-saving winches and the natural seamanship of the Åland Islanders, while plentiful rations and good officers made for contented sailors. Villiers felt he would be able to make up the sea-time for his ticket on this ship, but again fate intervened. Almost at the very end of the voyage, as the *Lawhill* approached her anchorage off Port Lincoln in South Australia on a dark night, she gently touched bottom with her bows. The ship sustained no damage, but Villiers, working aloft with both hands occupied, was thrown to the deck by the impact. He was lucky to be alive after such a fall, but his descent had been softened by rigging and no bones were broken. He had, however, received a deep wound in the thigh from a ringbolt against which he had fallen, and this immobilized him for months. As the *Lawhill* sailed on her way, Villiers was discharged and faced the prospect of the end of his sailing career. After a dispiriting interlude working in an iron foundry, and a short spell on a trading ketch that brought home to him that he was not yet physically strong enough for the sailing ship life, he signed on for a spell as an able seaman on board a tramp steamer.

His time on the 6,000 ton *Erriba* reinforced all his old prejudices against engine-powered ships and convinced him that the sea to him meant sail or nothing. Life aboard this 'clumsy lump', with its large crew, comfortable accommodation and excellent food, was a deadening and monotonous experience for which Villiers reserves his deepest scorn. The romance and challenge of the sea had been reduced to a life little different from a factory ashore, and the thought of a 'career of watchkeeping on some dull steamer's bridge' appalled him. Deeply despondent, in 1922 he left for Tasmania and a new life: 'Nineteen years old, with nothing to my credit but four years of wasted time trying to qualify for a profession I no longer considered worth following.'

After a series of odd jobs he eventually succeeded in becoming a journalist, but the sea was not so easily to be washed from his blood, and his new profession was soon to offer the resourceful Villiers a way of sailing in the ships he loved while earning a living. In 1923 he persuaded his employers at the *Hobart Mercury* to allow him to take a passage as a labourer on the *Sir James Clark Ross*, then heading for the Antarctic on the first modern whaling expedition to the Ross Sea. Villiers's account of the voyage, illustrated with his own photographs, was published as a series of articles and subsequently in book form as *Whaling in the Frozen South*. For the rest of his life he was able to use his writing skills to subsidize sailing ship ventures that would not otherwise have been possible.

As the sailing ships of the world steadily dwindled – whether through the challenge of steam, loss at sea, the breaker's yard or plain old age – Villiers conceived the idea of documenting their last days through word and image. Chance again played a hand while he was in Melbourne on business in December 1927. Lying in the basin was the big four-masted barque *Herzogin Cecilie*, and when he boarded her for a look around he found her master to be Ruben de Cloux, his captain from the old *Lawhill* days. On the spur of the moment, Villiers signed on as an able seaman at six (Australian) pounds a month for the voyage to England. *Herzogin Cecilie* was to race against the *Beatrice*, and Villiers hoped to make a book out of what was to be one of the last of the 'grain races'. The 15,000 mile race from Port Lincoln to the Lizard had all the makings of a gripping sea story, but not perhaps in the way Villiers had anticipated. Captain de Cloux was a legendary skipper, reputed to have the gift of conjuring up the winds and weather he wanted, but on this voyage everything was against him. The ship was severely undermanned and two of the mates were of poor quality. De Cloux pushed the ship hard through heavy weather that stretched the crew to the limits of endurance. But once round the Horn and nearing the Equator, they languished in the doldrums. Working the great ship to catch every whisper of wind was hard and demoralizing work, and in addition to his duties Villiers was writing and photographing. Falmouth was reached on the ninety-sixth day out, and to their astonishment they had beaten the *Beatrice*. Villiers had some difficulty finding a publisher for his account of the voyage, *Falmouth for Orders*, and after spending some time investigating the apple trade in Europe on behalf of his newspaper, he returned to Tasmania on the *Jervis Bay*.

Villiers's reports on the fruit trade in Europe had made his reputation as a journalist in Tasmania, but he was still unable to turn his back on the sea; in 1929 he signed on as an able seaman on the Finnish full-rigged ship *Grace Harwar* with fellow journalist Ronald Gregory Walker. Their plan was to record, through film, photographs and words, a voyage on one of the last of the sailing ships. *Grace Harwar* was chosen for her looks rather than her sailing abilities, since ships with brace-winches and other mechanical aids were not considered suitable in a film which planned to 'record the age-old fight of man against the sea'. In every other respect she was notorious, and 'her name was near the top of the list in my little book of ships not to sail in'. Someone was killed on nearly every voyage and for the previous two years her condition had been allowed to deteriorate. She was nearing the end of her career and therefore little money would be spent on her; but for all these defects, the unprotected open wheel and the heavy hand braces, 'she was the best ship in the fleet from the documentary point of view . . . no clipper, but an unspoiled old-timer'.

But, tragically, *Grace Harwar* fully lived up to her evil reputation:

> We were lucky to arrive at all. On the voyage Walker was killed, the second mate driven out of his mind, the ship sprang a serious leak, and we ran out of food . . . We were the last ship to sail and the last in the race. The whole voyage was a savage fight against the sea, in a ship which was seriously handicapped from the setting-out to the end . . .

Walker was killed by a falling spar, and Villiers carried on filming alone. All his efforts seemed to be mocked when at the end of the voyage, the 'boys of Wardour Street' who agreed to market his film insisted on making it into a feature, inventing a preposterous plot and ruthlessly excising any documentary value it possessed. But as so often in Villiers's life chance came to his aid. Dr Grosvenor of the National Geographic Society of Washington read about the film, and invited Villiers to lecture in America. A popular nationwide tour followed and with the success of his written account of the voyage, *By Way of Cape Horn*, which became a modest bestseller, Villiers found himself in the unfamiliar position of having capital at his disposal.

For a man of Villiers's stamp the use to which he must put this money was self-evident. Teaming up with Captain de Cloux, he sank his savings in the *Parma*, a four-masted steel barque of a little over 3,000 gross tons, built at Port Glasgow in 1902. This was not such an impulsive act as might be thought. They sailed the *Parma* to Australia in ballast at the end of 1931, and returned early in 1932 with a cargo of wheat that realized a profit of £3,000. A second voyage was also successful, with a run of eighty-three days from Port Victoria to Falmouth making it one of the fastest passages for half a century. While Villiers was an owner of the *Parma* he had sailed under Captain de Cloux, but now he felt himself sufficiently experienced for his own command. He sold back his share in the *Parma* and set out to find a ship.

This was the *Georg Stage*, seen up for sale at her moorings in Copenhagen harbour in 1934. For £1,500 she was his, although he was not yet quite sure how he was going to use her; but with that blend of optimism and recklessness that carried him through life, Villiers 'decided to make a voyage round the world, an ambling circumnavigation by way of

Good Hope and the Horn . . . and to ship all the young fellows who cared to come and there was room for'. For this adventure he renamed her *Joseph Conrad*, in homage to the great novelist of the sea, and whose own ship, the *Otago*, he used to see in Hobart, living out her days as a coal hulk. His vision of a sail training ship is perhaps the most concrete expression of his love of the old square-riggers, for much as he loved the beauty of these craft, his was not merely a sentimental attachment. If the sailing ship as an economic means of moving goods must inevitably fade away, it still had a role to play in teaching self-reliance and a spirit of community, and in instilling a sense of achievement in mastering complex and difficult tasks. But after two years and a successful journey round the world, his liabilities had accumulated and he was forced to sell her to a rich young man who planned to turn her into a yacht, 'the kind of ship I most detested, the good ship turned into a harlot . . .'

As European sail died away he turned to other cultures in 'a programme . . . by which I hoped to acquaint myself with the sailing-vessels of the world . . . A life of wandering in sailing-ships appealed to me, and I proposed to make an exhaustive survey of the types of ships and trades I came across, and to photograph and make films as records'. First came the dhows of the Red Sea and Indian Ocean, with whom Villiers lived and sailed until, just as he was negotiat-

ing the purchase of a Kuwaiti *baggala*, the Second World War burst upon the world.

The war – in which he served with distinction as a commander of landing craft in several theatres – formed a turning point in Villiers's career, for at its end the era of the great sailing ships had indeed ended. His contact with the sea was maintained as an adviser to film projects such as *Moby Dick*, and as captain of the *Mayflower* replica which made a historic crossing of the Atlantic in 1957. But if the great European age of sail was over, there were still other cultures to explore, whether sailing in a Maldives *buggalow* or exploring the Brahmaputra. To the end of his life Villiers travelled, sailed and photographed the diminishing heritage of the world's sailing fleets, and he died in 1982 after a life immersed in all aspects of the sea. His photographic record of his life and the ships he sailed in, together with his writings, form perhaps the single most important surviving documentation of the last days of sail. And through all his wandering life there runs that same refrain of reverence for the sea and deep respect for all those who make their lives upon the oceans of the world, whether through choice or force of circumstance. His own life, and his love of the sea, is perhaps best summed up in his own verdict on the cruise of the *Joseph Conrad*: 'I had sailed her round the world and had lost no life, and hurt nobody. I had kept my ideals and stood no nonsense.'

Opposite: **Going aloft on the *Parma*, 1932–3**
Photograph by Alan Villiers

Left: **View along the main deck of the *Parma*, 1932–3**
Photograph by Alan Villiers

Originally named *Arrow*, the *Parma* had been built for the Anglo-American Oil Company in 1902 to transport case-oil between New York and the Far East; she had the largest unobstructed hold of any sailing ship afloat and a cargo capacity of over 5,000 tons. Villiers owned nineteen-hundredths of her from 1931 to 1933, and made a good profit on his investment from the voyages she made carrying grain between Australia and Europe in this period.

View from the mizzen mast of the *Grace Harwar*, 1929
Photograph by Alan Villiers

Built in 1889, the *Grace Harwar* was owned by Gustaf Erikson from 1916 until 1935, when she was broken up. This dramatic view of white water sweeping across her deck as she neared Cape Horn was taken during the ill-fated voyage in which Villiers's friend Ronald Gregory Walker was killed in a fall from the rigging.

Below: **Seaman at the helm of the *Herzogin Cecilie*, 1928**
Photograph by Alan Villiers
The *Herzogin Cecilie* encountered some very heavy weather during the first half of her 1928 voyage from Melbourne to Falmouth with a cargo of grain, but this photograph was evidently taken during the long and disheartening period when the ship languished in the doldrums as she approached the Equator. At ninety-six days, she had still managed a better performance than any of the other ships involved in the Grain Race of that year, several of which took up to 120 days to make the passage.

Opposite above: **The *Parma* weighing anchor, 1932–3**
Photograph by Alan Villiers
Although she was, in Villiers's words, 'an enormous sailing-ship', the *Parma* 'sailed very well and was comfortable and dry in ballast. She was also surprisingly light to handle. She steered well, and had a fine whaleback wheelhouse to protect the helmsman . . . a pleasant, sea-kindly ship.' The eight men seen here are working the capstan on the forecastle head.

Opposite below: **Pulley haul on board the *Parma*, 1933**
Photograph by Alan Villiers
Parma's 1933 passage from South Australia to Falmouth with a cargo of grain valued at about £7,400 was, at eighty-three days, the fastest voyage made by any of the ships engaged in the Grain Races between Europe and Australia.

Above: **Crew working in heavy seas on the *Parma*, 1932–3**
Photograph by Alan Villiers
The watch works knee-deep in water sweeping across the main deck of the *Parma* as she approaches Cape Horn: 'At last!' wrote Villiers in his journal, 'The real Cape Horn wind – roaring gale and roaring sea, hail and sleet and snow, and the old ship shortened down and foaming on . . . She ships some heavy water now, particularly when a great sea thunders over her 'midships and breaks halfway to the crojack yard. She steers hard in the squalls and the helm will not go up; but she runs splendidly at twelve knots and everyone is pleased . . .'

Opposite: **Looking aloft on board the *Parma*, 1933**
Photograph by Alan Villiers
This photograph is taken from the outer end of the bowsprit looking aloft towards the foremast, where members of the crew are taking in sail. The lower topgallant has been taken in and the men are in the process of furling the upper topgallant sail.

Taking a bath on the deck of the *Herzogin Cecilie*, 1928
Photograph by Alan Villiers
Crew members take a welcome shower, improvised from an oil-drum, on the well deck of the *Herzogin Cecilie*. This ship was owned by Gustaf Erikson from 1921 until 1936, when she was wrecked due to navigational error in fog off Salcombe in Devon.

Opposite: **Sunbathing on the *Parma*, 1933**
Photograph by Hilgard Pannes
This view shows boys relaxing in the forecastle head while the *Parma* was at anchor off Port Victoria at the start of the 1933 passage. The photograph was taken on Villiers's camera by Hilgard Pannes, a Long Island youth serving his sailing apprenticeship on board the ship.

Opposite above: **Scraping the deck of the *Parma*, 1932–3**
Photograph by Alan Villiers
The onset of easy sailing weather was not a period of relaxation for the seaman, but merely the opportunity to attend to an unending list of chores needed to keep a ship seaworthy. As Villiers wrote of this voyage: 'If there were not the sails to look after, there was the ship. All of the running rigging required attention, and the standing rigging, too. She was to be surveyed on arrival in England, and there were many minor repairs to be seen to before they met the surveyor's eagle eye. The decks were repaired; the steel bulwarks scrubbed and scraped and red-leaded and painted, and then washed every morning; the brace winches overhauled, and the braces; the rigging tarred down and the lower masts painted. Each day began at six a.m.'

Opposite below: **Loading cargo into the *Herzogin Cecilie*, Port Lincoln, South Australia, 1928**
Photograph by Alan Villiers
Herzogin Cecilie's cargo of grain is being loaded from railway trucks on the quayside, a few days before her departure on 19 January 1928 on the ninety-six-day passage to Falmouth.

Above: **Model-making on board the *Parma*, 1932–3**
Photograph by Alan Villiers
Ship model-making has been a source of recreation for sailors down the ages. This young crew member, so far unidentified, is constructing a model of the *Parma*.

ACKNOWLEDGEMENTS

The photographers of many of the illustrations in a book of this sort are inevitably unknown. The following list, however, locates in alphabetical order the work of identified photographers:

Bedford Lemère 36, 68–9, 70–71, 71 *(right)*, 72 *(top)*, 78, 80 *(top)*, 80 *(bottom)*, 81, 82 *(top)*, 82 *(bottom)*; **Bonfils** 125 *(top)*; **Borgiotti** 125 *(bottom)*; **Nicholas Caire**, 119; **Samuel Clifford** 118 *(bottom)*; **Joseph Cundall** 66 *(bottom)*; **William McG. Eager** 43, 46 *(top)*, 48; **Roger Fenton** 143; **Francis Frith & Co.** 49 *(bottom)*, 54, 55, 57 *(top)*, 60, 62, 63 *(top)*, 63 *(bottom)*, 64 *(bottom)*, 94, 95, 136; **Gibson of Penzance** 10, 26, 27, 30–31, 85, 92; **Gould & Co.** 50, 51 *(top)*, 51 *(bottom)*; **E. Hopkins** 154 *(bottom)*; **Reverend Richard Calvert Jones** 15 *(top)*, 15 *(bottom)*, (?) 128; **G.R. Lambert & Co.** 117 *(bottom)*; **G. Miller** 98, **Francis Mortimer** 28 *(top)*, 129; **Eadweard Muybridge** 110; **Simeon H. Parsons** 112, 113 *(top)*, 113 *(bottom)*; **Charles Pickering** 34–5; **Herbert Ponting** 156, 170–75; **James Randall** 24; **Royal Engineers** 111 *(top)*; **William L.H. Skeen & Co.** 105, 123; **Paul Stabler** 16 *(top)*; **Stretton** 122 *(top)*; **Stuart** 139, 141 *(top)*, 141 *(bottom)*; **Frank M. Sutcliffe** 56;

William Henry Fox Talbot 44 *(top)*; **James Valentine** 57 *(bottom)*; **Alan Villiers** 25 *(top)*, 176–91; **Russell Westwood** 2; **George White or Thomas Mitchell** 162–5; **W. Fisk Williams or Wagentreiber** 122 *(below)*; **George Washington Wilson** 90–91.

The photographs in this book, except where otherwise noted, are reproduced by kind permission of the Director and Trustees of the National Maritime Museum. Many colleagues in the Museum have supplied information and guidance in the preparation of this work, but special thanks are due to Bob Todd and David Hodge of the Historic Photographs Section, who gave freely of both their time and their expert knowledge of the collections in their charge. Copying and printing of the photographs was organized and undertaken by the Museum Photographic Studio, and the work of David Spence, James Stevenson, Tina Chambers and Paul Eling in this respect is gratefully acknowledged. Finally, thanks are due to a former colleague, Denis Stonham, for making available his specialized knowledge of maritime history.

REFERENCES

The National Maritime Museum is able to supply prints from the photographs in its collections. The following list gives negative numbers of the illustrations used in this book, except in a few instances where copyright restrictions are in force:

Jacket front N61502; **jacket back** G10689; **page 2** P39690; **11** C4434; **15** *(top)* C5371; **15** *(bottom)* C2254; **16** *(top)* 5880; **16** *(bottom)* 8454; **17** 3133; **18** *(top)* P692; **18** *(bottom)* 6562; **19** A3105; **20** 4685; **21** *(top)* P39519; **21** *(bottom)* C4424; **22–3** P8236; **24** P 7145; **25** *(top)* N61563; **25** *(bottom)* P39478; **28** *(top)* P7633; **28** *(bottom)* P940; B5782; **32** *(top)* C1057/B; **32** *(bottom)* C1057/A; **33** P3119; **35** *(bottom)* P39480; **36** G10689; **37** P39524; **43** P27576; **44** *(top)* 4402; **44** *(bottom)* P140; **45** 6660; **46** P27565; **47** G3690–91; **48** P27550; **49** *(top)* P72139; **49** *(bottom)* G2794; **50** G116; **51** *(top)* G882; **51** *(bottom)* G931; **52** P39542; **53** P39541; **54** G3019; **55** G3274; **56** P39491; **57** *(top)* G3304; **57** *(bottom)* D4456/1; **58** P39533; **59** *(top)* P24678; **59** *(bottom)* P39552; **60** G3168; **61** G2850; **62** G2519; **63** *(top)* G3123; **63** *(bottom)* G2783; **64** *(top)* P39551; **64** *(bottom)* G3071; **65** *(top)* G3614; **65** *(bottom)* B8633; **66** *(top)* 3758; **66** *(bottom)* D676; **67** D1750; **68–9** G10583; **70–71** G10712; **71** G10917; **72** *(top)* G10547; **72** *(bottom)* D1752; **73** B5097; **74** *(top)* P39600; **74** *(bottom)* G12866; **75** G9900; **76** P28490; **77** C2973; **78** G10791; **79** *(top)* C7206/A; **79** *(bottom)* C4880/14; **80** *(top)* G10514; **80** *(bottom)* G10543; **81** G10781; **82** *(top)* P39543; **82** *(bottom)* P39544; **83** D5413/3; **84** N21886; **85** P39531; **90** D4456/10; **91** *(top)* P24701; **91** *(bottom)* P39482; **92** P39525; **93** P39526; **94** G3186; **95** G3491; **96** *(top)* HOH2; **96** *(bottom)* B1992/G; **97** 7055; **98** 5984; **99** P60305; **100** *(top left)* P39599; **100** *(top right)* P39597; **100** *(bottom left)* C6176; **100** *(bottom right)* P39594; **101** *(top)* P39595; **101** *(bottom)* P39598; **102** *(top)* G3631; **102** *(bottom)* G4234; **103** P39513; **104** P39479; **110** C4384; **111** *(top)* P39486; **111** *(bottom)* P39538; **112** P39483; **113** *(top)* P39484; **113** *(bottom)* P39485; **114** *(top)* P39554; **114** *(bottom)* P39562; **115** P39567; **117** *(bottom)* D2788; **118** *(top)* A8573/G; **118** *(bottom)* P39487; **119** P39488; **121** *(top)* B1979/D; **121** *(bottom)* A9635/C; **122** *(top)* P39489; **122** *(bottom)* P125; **123** P39490; **124** P39537; **125** *(top)* D2060; **125** *(bottom)* B6539; **128** C3607; **129** P39492; **133** A658; **134** A621/19; **135** *(top)* A621/27; **135** *(bottom)* P39593; **136** G3232; **137** P39549; **138** *(top)* P39575; **138** *(bottom)* P39509; **139** 4733; **140** N21763; **141** *(top)* A2221; **141** *(bottom)* 4736; **142** A2255; **143** C3953; **144** *(top)* P39547; **144** *(bottom)* P39574; **145** C5861; **146** A2201; **147** G10177; **148** A7534/13; **149** P39564; **150** P39545; **151** P39568; **152–3** A2239; **154** *(top)* N47745; **154** *(bottom)* N9713; **155** P39570; **156** P39493; **157** P39602; **162** P39586; **163** *(top)* P39592; **163** *(bottom)* P39585; **164** P39584; **165** *(top)* P39589; **165** *(bottom)* P39588; **166** *(top)* C8465/6; **166** *(bottom)* C8465/7; **167** C8465/24; **168** *(top)* P39577; **168** *(bottom)* P38641; **169** C8465/18; **170** P39495; **171** P39494; **172** *(top)* P39496; **172** *(bottom)* P39558; **173** P39497; **174** P39559; **175** *(top)* P39498; **175** *(bottom)* P39560; **176** N61549; **177** N61653; **181** N61533; **182** N61437; **183** N61319; **184** N61075; **185** *(top)* N61520; **185** *(bottom)* N61572; **186** N61484; **187** N61744; **188** N61612; **189** N61099; **190** *(top)* N61600; **190** *(bottom)* N61087; **191** N61643.